WAR IN THE VILLAGES

WAR IN THE VILLAGES

The U.S. Marine Corps Combined Action Platoons in the Vietnam War

by
Ted N. Easterling

Number 5 in the American Military Studies Series

University of North Texas Press
Denton, Texas

Printed in the United States of America.

10 9 8 7 6 5 4 3 2

Permissions:
University of North Texas Press
1155 Union Circle #311336
Denton, TX 76203-5017

The paper used in this book meets the minimum requirements of the American National Standard for Permanence of Paper for Printed Library Materials, z39.48.1984. Binding materials have been chosen for durability.

Library of Congress Cataloging-in-Publication Data

Easterling, Ted N., 1946– author.
War in the villages : the U.S. Marine Corps combined action platoons in the Vietnam War / Ted N. Easterling.
American military studies ; no. 5.
Denton, Texas : University of North Texas Press, [2021]
pages cm
Includes bibliographical references and index.
ISBN-13 978-1-57441-826-2 (cloth), 978-1-57441-994-8 (paper)
ISBN-13 978-1-57441-834-7 (ebook)
1. LCSH: United States. Marine Corps. Combined Action Program—History. 2. United States. Marine Corps—History—Vietnam War, 1961–1975. 3. Vietnam War, 1961–1975—Underground movements. 4. Counterinsurgency—Vietnam—History—20th century. 5. Combined operations. (Military science)—History—20th century.

DS558.4 .E37 2021
959.704/34–dc23

2020051339

War in the Villages: The U. S. Marine Corps Combined Action Platoons in the Vietnam War is Number 5 in the American Military Studies Series

The electronic edition of this book was made possible by the support of the Vick Family Foundation. Typeset by vPrompt eServices.

I would first like to dedicate this book to the memory of my mother and my father, Rachel Hollys Easterling and George Riley Easterling. I also dedicate it to my wife, Mary E. Quinn, and my family. Among my family members, I especially dedicate it to Riley Grace Goch, who always has a smile to make me feel better.
Last, I dedicate this book to the memory of my friend, Guy Richard Barattieri.

Contents

Acknowledgments

I would like to thank Dr. Walter L. Hixson for his help in completing this book. Without his advice and help it would not have been possible. My friend Dr. Larry Fallis read my manuscript and gave me the encouragement I needed to complete the project. Among my friends who gave me support were John Wunderle, Tom Paskert, John Kordinak, Bill Eckels, and Joe Green. At various times a few words from each of you helped me more than you know. My accomplishing this work is due to your help.

My editor Ron Chrisman was more patient than he should have been, and I appreciate him for that. The Archives Branch, Marine Corps History Division always gave me tremendous help in my research. The technical help Marj and Bruce Hurst gave me made this book possible. Finally, I want to thank all the people on the CAP Marine History-Vietnam website for helping me with this. I would not have expected less of Marines.

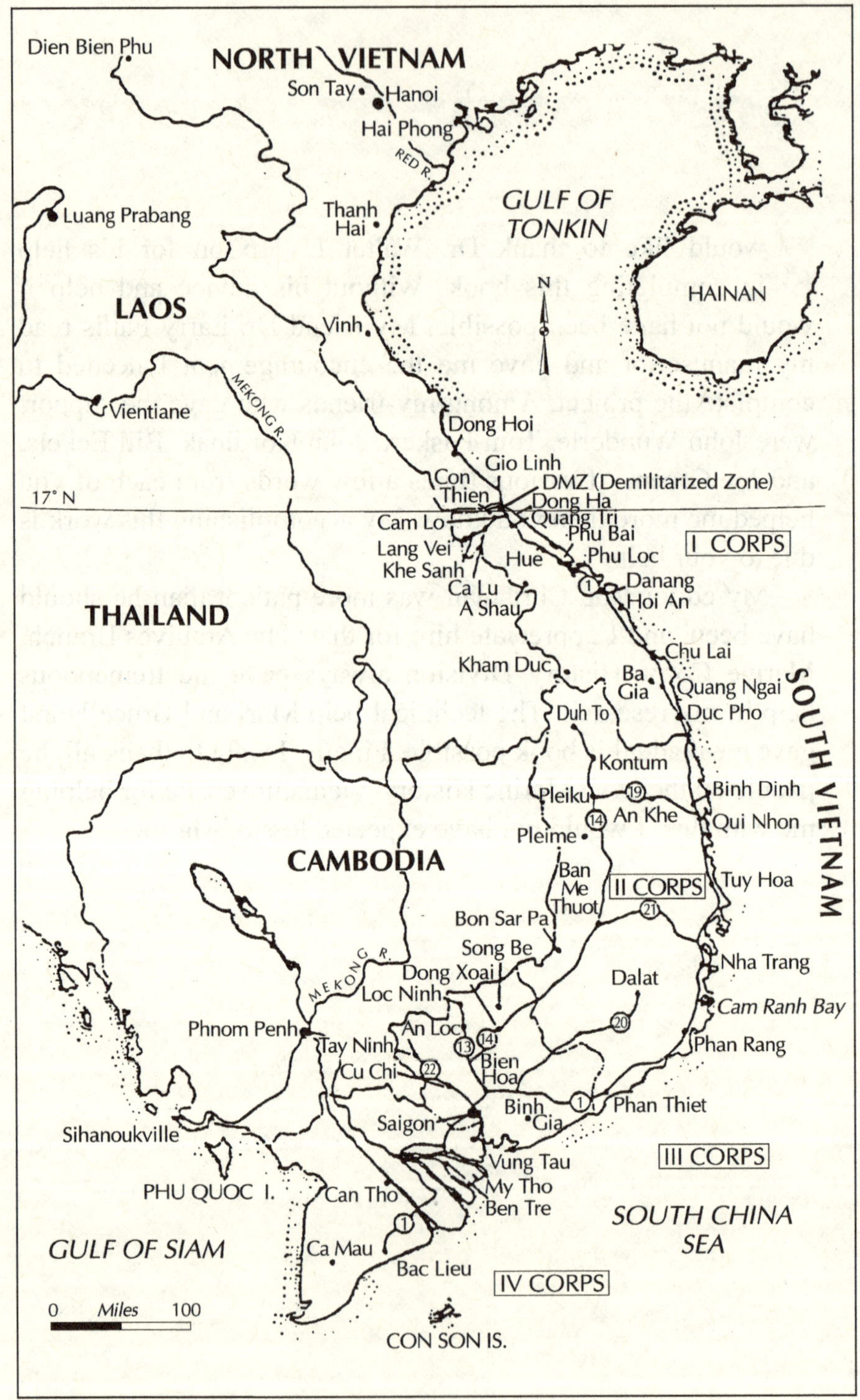

Map 1 Indochina

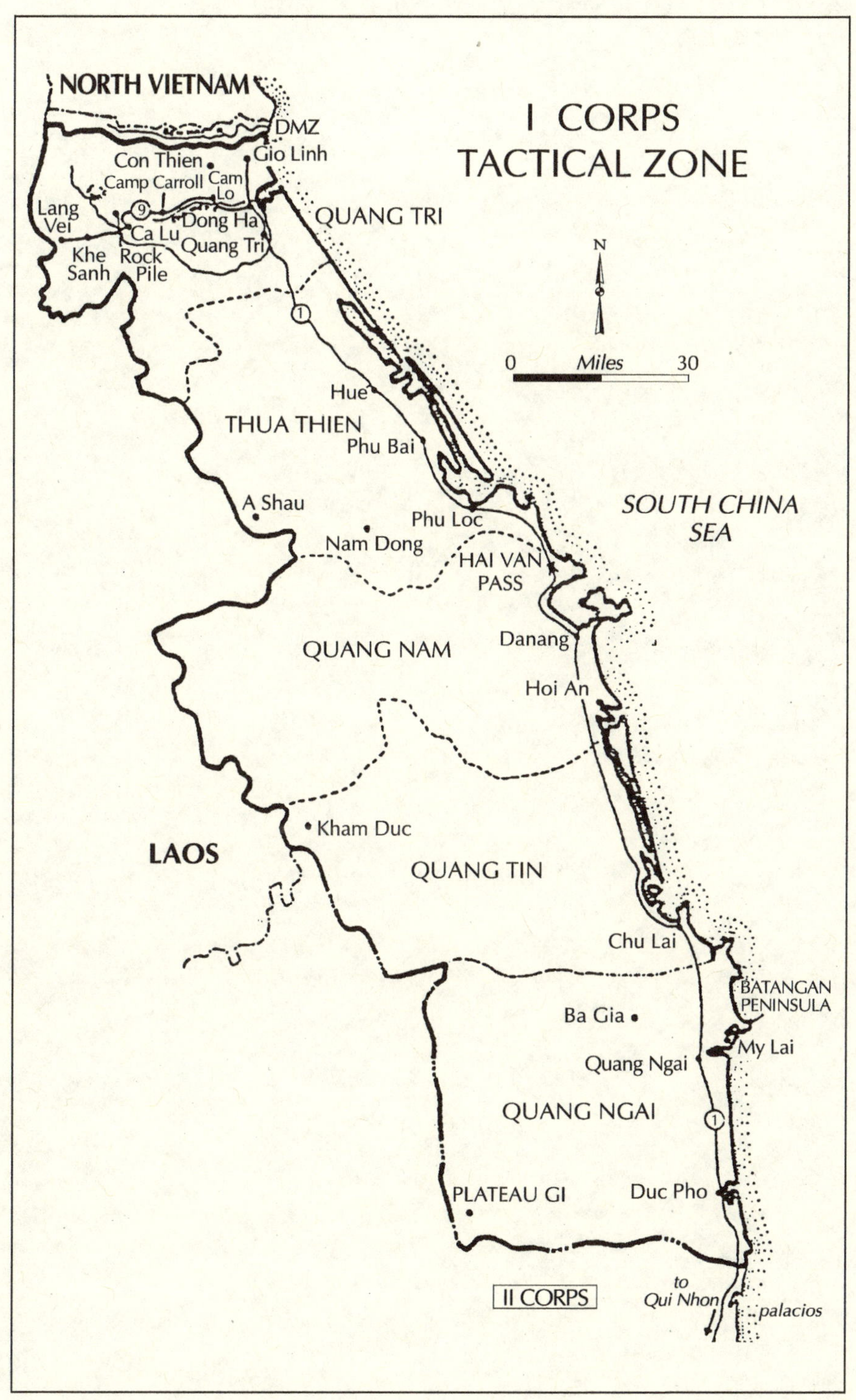

Map 2 Military Region I

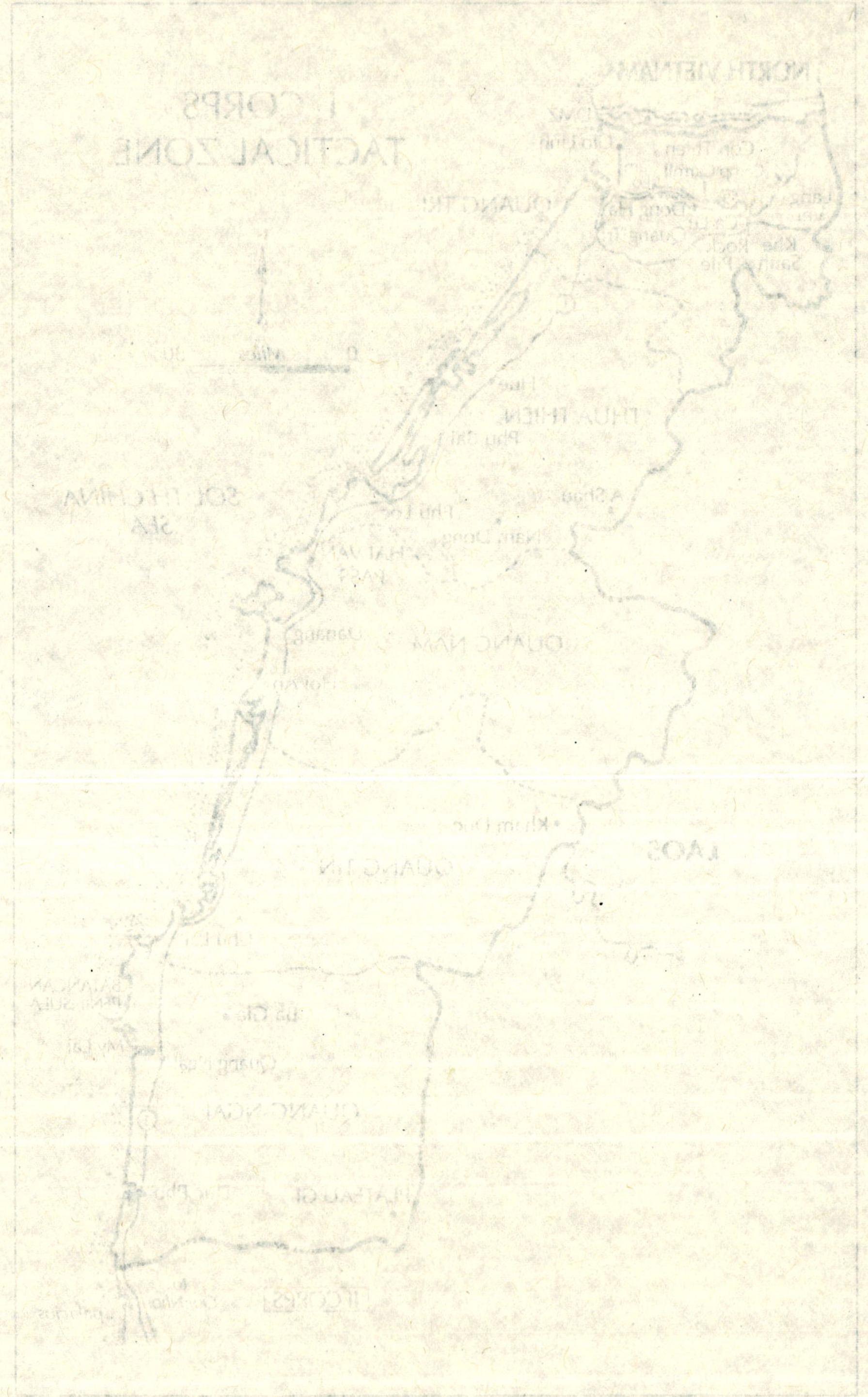

Introduction

Near the middle of September 1966, a mixed force of approximately one hundred and fifty North Vietnamese Army (NVA) regulars and National Liberation Front (NLF) fighters conducted a night attack on the fortified compound where the Combined Action Platoon (CAP) was headquartered, and the CAP was overrun. At the time of the attack there were only six Marines, a Navy corpsman, and twelve Vietnamese Popular Forces (PF) militiamen in the compound because the other Marines and PFs had gone out on patrols earlier in the evening. A reaction force of Marine infantrymen eventually arrived, and they and the other CAP members forced the NVA and NLF forces to retreat, but the assault was fast and overwhelming. Five of the six Marines and the corpsman were killed in the battle, and the sixth Marine was wounded.[1] Seven of the PFs managed to hold off the enemy to some degree during the fight, and the other five PFs were wounded. The results of the fight were a brutal example of how vulnerable unassisted CAPs were to an attack by a large enemy forcc.

In the aftermath of the battle, the surviving Marines demonstrated their determination to remain in the village. The morning after the assault General Lowell English, commander of the First Marine Division, came to the location and spoke with the six CAP Marines who had survived because they were on patrols when the attack began. The general told the men the mission the CAP was given may have been too much for such a small force, and it might be better to have a platoon of regular Marine infantry patrol the area. In effect, English was telling the men they could leave if they wanted. All the Marines said they wanted to stay. Later one of the Marines said, "What would we have said to the PFs after the way we pushed them to fight the Cong? We had to stay. There wasn't one of us who wanted to leave." English accepted the men's decision and told them he would make sure they were sent six excellent volunteers as replacements for the men killed and wounded in the fight.[2]

That afternoon, funeral services were conducted at a small Buddhist pagoda close to the marketplace for the five Americans and the six Vietnamese CAP members killed in the battle. Before the funeral the Buddhist monks went to the compound and asked the Marines to join them, and the Marines did. The large funeral procession wound through the village, and the monks mentioned the names of both the Vietnamese and the Americans when they prayed for the dead. After the funeral the Marines thanked the people for their prayers and for their expressions of sorrow, and they then returned to the compound.[3]

On the night after the compound was overrun, the NLF returned to reclaim the village. The PFs heard from the people that the NLF said the CAP was defeated, the Marines were leaving, and the NLF guerrillas were returning to the village that night. CAP patrols were sent out, and one soon ran into a large force of guerrillas near the marketplace. In the ensuing fight the patrol was quickly reinforced by Marines and PFs from the compound, and by a Marine infantry reaction force. In the hard fight the guerrillas were defeated, and they suffered significant casualties. The CAP demonstrated it lost a battle when the compound was overrun, but it was not defeated, and the CAP would stay in the village.[4]

This incident is one small piece of the history of the US Marine Corps Combined Action Platoons in the Vietnam War. The platoons were mixed groups of Marines and South Vietnamese Popular Forces militia who lived and worked together in some of the villages of South Vietnam. Part of the mission of these small groups of approximately fifty men was to defend the villages from the NLF and the NVA. Duty in the CAPs could be both dangerous and monotonous. Death might come in a close, vicious fight in the ink-black of a Vietnamese night after weeks of uneventful patrolling, or it could come in the surprise of a massive NLF attack.

The heroism and the dedication of the Marines who volunteered to serve in these units is commendable, but the very existence of these platoons raises some questions. First, of course, what could possess Marines to volunteer for something this dangerous? Also, was there a larger purpose for the CAPs than simply defending a few villages from the guerrillas? Importantly, if there was a larger purpose for the CAPs, how well did they accomplish that purpose?

The thinking behind the creation of the CAPs was to more effectively fight the NLF by using the strengths of the Marines to improve the PF militia, and by using the strengths of the PFs to improve the Marines. Some of the strengths the Marines brought to the platoons were their discipline, their professionalism, and their firepower. For their part, the men of the PF platoons were invaluable to the Marines in many ways. The Vietnamese knew the surrounding area, the people of the village, and the enemy. They could guide the Marines on the patrols the platoons conducted, they knew which villagers were friendly, they knew which families had relatives among the NLF, and they knew the habits and the fighting techniques of the NLF. As the Marines and the PFs lived together in the villages they came to know each other, and the Vietnamese gave the Marines a better understanding of the culture and of the language of Vietnam.[5]

This study will fill a gap in existing research by using counterinsurgency principles to analyze CAP performance as a counterinsurgency concept in the Vietnam War. Little has been written about the performance of the Combined Action Platoons in the Vietnam War, and even less has been written about the CAPs as a concept of counterinsurgency. Using counterinsurgency ideas to evaluate the CAP performance during the Vietnam War will help show whether the CAP program might have been a fundamental piece of a successful, general counterinsurgency strategy in the war. Also, it may show that this thinking is misguided, and that the CAPs have been overrated in their performance and their potential as a counterinsurgency technique. In either event, evaluating the CAPs as a counterinsurgency concept will help resolve some of the differences between those who think a more conventional approach was best in the war, and those who think a counterinsurgency approach would have brought about better results.

The strategy used by the United States in the Vietnam War is important for this study of the CAP program. There are two types of strategy which need to be defined, and the first of these is national strategy. National strategy can be defined as, "The art and science of developing and using the political, economic, and psychological powers of a nation, together with its armed forces, during peace and war, to secure national objectives."[6] The national strategy of the United States in the Republic of Vietnam was detailed in a National Security Action Memorandum approved by President Lyndon Johnson on November 26, 1963. This memorandum stated the "central object of the United States in South Vietnam is to assist the people and Government of that country to win their contest against the externally directed and supported Communist conspiracy."[7] The second type of strategy is military strategy, which can be defined as "The art and science of employing the armed forces of a nation to secure the objectives of national policy by the application of force, or the threat of force."[8] When the United States committed ground combat forces to fight the war in Vietnam in March 1965, a military strategy was conceived to fulfill the US strategic objectives in Vietnam.

Much of the warfare conducted by the NLF and the NVA in the Vietnam War was basically guerrilla warfare. Guerrilla warfare is the method of warfare counterinsurgency is intended to fight, and so it is necessary to understand it to analyze the effectiveness of the CAP program as a counterinsurgency method. Also, because counterinsurgency is a method of warfare used to fight against guerrilla warfare, some of the fundamental ideas of counterinsurgency warfare need to be discussed to evaluate the CAP program as a counterinsurgency concept in the war.

Guerrilla warfare is one of the oldest methods of warfare, and it is one of the best ways for a weaker force to fight a stronger enemy. The guerrillas can hide from a larger and a better-equipped army and strike quickly at supply columns and inattentive groups of soldiers. The guerrillas can disperse in a moment when the enemy attacks, or when the enemy is too strong. A primary rule for guerrillas is to retreat before strength, and to attack weakness.

One of the most important points in understanding guerrilla warfare is to realize guerrillas depend on the people for their existence, and because of this the guerrillas need the support of a significant percentage of the local population if they are to be successful. In many situations, guerrillas avoid detection by government troops by posing as civilians to blend in with the local civilian population. Also, the guerrillas frequently hide in remote camps to avoid opposing forces. In these and other situations the guerrillas depend on the people not to betray them.

In addition, the guerrillas usually depend almost exclusively on the people of the local population for food, intelligence, recruits, and supplies. For these reasons a guerrilla movement cannot exist without the support of a substantial number of the people in a country.[9]

Communism offered a revolutionary ideology which changed guerrilla warfare in the twentieth century. In the Chinese Civil War, Mao Zedong blended the political ideology of communism and concepts from Chinese military classics with guerrilla war to conceive the potent hybrid of revolutionary warfare. Mao saw the political indoctrination of the people as critical for the success of revolutionary warfare. His objective was the creation of a communist state, "Without a political goal, guerrilla warfare must fail," he declared, "as it must if its political objectives do not coincide with the aspirations of the people and their sympathy, cooperation, and assistance cannot be gained."[10] He emphasized the importance of the people for the guerrillas when he said, "Many people think it impossible for guerrillas to exist for long in the enemy's rear. Such a belief reveals lack of comprehension of the relationship that should exist between the people and the troops. The former may be likened to water and the latter to the fish who inhabit it."[11] This allegiance of the people was gained partly through relentless political education of the people. Propaganda was so important because a new society with a new ideology was the objective. In the introduction to Mao Zedong's book, *On Guerrilla Warfare*, Samuel B. Griffith, the translator, said, "A revolutionary war is never confined within the bounds of military action. Because its purpose is to destroy an existing society and its institutions and to replace them with a completely new state structure, any revolutionary war is a unity of which the constituent parts, in varying importance, are military, political, economic, social, and psychological."[12]

So, the attack of revolutionary war on a society was not exclusively military; instead, it was a political, economic, social, and psychological attack on the existing society. Because of this the military attack of the guerrillas might be contained, but the war could be lost in the end because of the erosion of the existing society by the success of the economic, social, and psychological elements of revolutionary war. This was an elusive quality of revolutionary war which made it an especially powerful form of guerrilla warfare.

The Vietnamese used revolutionary warfare with stunning results when they overthrew French colonial control during the French Indochinese War (1946–1954), and, also, in the Vietnam War. Of the guerrilla wars during the post-World War II period, the Chinese model of revolutionary war was probably used in its purest form outside of China in these two conflicts. General Vo Nguyen Giap of the NVA showed the similarity of his thinking to Mao Zedong's teachings of revolutionary war when he wrote, "Not only did we fight in the military field but also in the political, economic, and cultural field." He went on to say, "In the cultural field, we had to develop the culture of the Resistance imbued with a mass character and to heighten patriotism and hatred…."[13] There were some changes as a result of the circumstances of the wars, but for the most part the Vietnamese followed the Chinese pattern of revolutionary warfare during both the French Indochinese War and the Vietnam War.

Revolutionary warfare generally has three phases, and for the most part the NLF and the NVA used these three phases during the Vietnam War. In the initial defensive phase, the revolutionary cadres teach the people the political principles of the revolution and the cadres develop a political infrastructure network among the people. The second phase uses guerrilla warfare to expand the geographical area and the percentage of the population under the control of the revolution. As the revolution gains more control over the land and the population of the country it gains access to more of the food, recruits, and intelligence that guerrilla forces need to exist and to succeed. Also, during this phase main force units of battalion size are trained and equipped, but these units are seldom used in combat.[14] Instead, they are formed primarily for use in the third stage of the revolution. The third phase of revolutionary warfare starts after the revolutionary forces grow in strength to achieve a rough parity between their forces and those of the government. At this point the guerrillas continue to fight the government army, but now the main force battalions organized during the second phase confront the government forces in open combat to take complete control of the country.[15]

A guerrilla war is frequently a formidable challenge, and counterinsurgency is a method of warfare a government in power uses to fight an insurgency. There are variations, but there are two basic strategies for a counterinsurgency war. The first of these is to use overwhelming and indiscriminate force to kill as many of the guerrillas and the people who support them as possible. In doing this, many homes, farms, and businesses are destroyed, and many innocent people are also killed. The objective of this approach is to destroy the guerrillas and to destroy their means of subsistence, and it is also meant to create such fear of the government that none of the people will support the insurgency.[16] Apart from the ethical questions inherent in this policy, creating a fear of the government also creates a great hatred of the government. The government can never have any trust in the people after this, and if the government becomes weak it is probable the insurgency will start again.

The second basic approach is to fight a counterinsurgency war as if it were a mirror of the insurgency. The insurgency has an ideological base which challenges the ideology of the government in power, and the government attacks the ideology of the insurgency. The allegiance of the people of the country is seen as the true prize and strength for both sides.[17] The ideological appeal of the insurgency has political, economic, social, and psychological elements, and the counterinsurgency needs to find ways to neutralize and discredit each of these. Social, economic, and political reforms are among the ways this can be done. Also, propaganda, which may include appeals such as those to historical patriotism and traditional values, can be used. The use of military force is the smallest element in this approach. The army systematically clears the populated areas of guerrillas and then uses its forces to prevent the guerrillas from returning. In doing this, the army is careful not to harm the people as it pursues the guerrillas, and the soldiers are trained to treat the people of the country well. Winning the support of the people and keeping them physically separated from the guerrillas is the most important part of this approach to pacification. Without the support of the people, and access to the people, the guerrillas lose the supplies, the intelligence, and the recruits needed for the existence of the insurgency.[18]

The reality of counterinsurgency is usually somewhere between the more brutal and the more benign examples of counterinsurgency warfare described here. However, it is usually more similar to the brutal example. Some persuasion of the people may be attempted, but terror, intimidation, and indiscriminate killing quickly become the rule. The military historian Douglas Porch put it well when he said counterinsurgency warfare techniques "place the crosshairs on the people in a process of escalation inherent in war and are seldom population-friendly. The people are not so much biddable as they become targets of force and coercion, and the competition devolves not into one of governance but into intimidation by both sides…."[19] The truth is that much of the nature of any war is simply a matter of vicious killing, and this is especially true of guerrilla war. Fighting enemies who hide among people who frequently support them and suffering losses from ambushes, snipers, and booby traps can become insanely frustrating. It is all too easy and seemingly effective to lash out with mindless brutality.

Much of this was true for the Vietnam War, but it was not true for all of it. There was a good deal of idealism in the effort of the US in Vietnam, despite the overall catastrophic effect of the Indochinese war. Many of the pacification programs in the war were intended to help the people. Most of the Americans who fought in Vietnam thought they were helping the people of a weak country defend themselves from totalitarian aggression, and they were sincere in their desire to help the people while they were there. The CAPs may or may not be an example of these more humane attempts on the part of the United States. If they were, and if they were an effective counterinsurgency concept in Vietnam, it might be reasoned that a more effective counterinsurgency war which truly tried to help the people could have been fought in Vietnam if the program had been handled differently. This is a question which needs more discussion, and it will be addressed here.

In counterinsurgency warfare the primary objective is not to destroy the opposing army or capture the enemy's capital; the objective in counterinsurgency warfare is to gain the loyalty of the people. The counterinsurgency theorist John Nagl stated the importance of gaining the loyalty of the population when he wrote, "An insurgency is a competition between insurgent and government for the support of the civilian population, which provides the sea in which the insurgents swim."[20]

The counterinsurgency functions used to evaluate how well the CAP units worked as a concept during the Vietnam War were chosen from counterinsurgency theory for their ability to gain the loyalty of the people and defeat the insurgents. The principles used were current at the time of the Vietnam War, and they are based on the ideas of the theorists David Galula and Robert Thompson. The most important task was to provide security for the people by fighting the guerrillas to keep them out of the villages and away from the people. While they worked to keep the guerrillas away from the villages it was important for the

CAPs to prevent the guerrillas from obtaining food, supplies, recruits, and intelligence information from the villagers. The CAP members needed to gain the goodwill and the loyalty of the people and develop intelligence sources among the villagers. As part of their intelligence work, the CAPs had to find and eliminate any guerrilla agents or members of the guerrilla infrastructure among the people of the villages. Another task for the CAPs was the performance of civic action and economic development projects to improve the living conditions of the villages. This would give the people better living conditions in the present in contrast to the guerrillas' promises of a better life in the future. Psychological operations needed to be conducted to discredit the guerrillas and to promote the loyalty of the people to the central government. Local government also needed to be developed and strengthened with the intention of improving the control of the central government over the villages.

Washington gave US Army General William Westmoreland responsibility for choosing a military strategy for the war, and he decided on a military strategy of attrition. One important reason he chose this strategy was that the US government wanted to confine the war to South Vietnam. Even though the war in South Vietnam was almost entirely directed and supported by North Vietnam, the US did not want to invade North Vietnam and risk a confrontation with the Chinese such as had occurred in the Korean War. Westmoreland also chose a strategy of attrition because he thought the NVA and the NLF had progressed to the third phase of revolutionary warfare. Main force units of the NVA and the NLF were fighting pitched battles with the ARVN in an effort to topple the government of South Vietnam, and in Westmoreland's opinion these main force units were a constant threat, and they needed to be defeated before full attention could be turned to pacification. The objective of this military strategy of attrition was to kill NVA and NLF main force unit troops until the NLF and

North Vietnam either lost the will to resist, or they were unable to field an effective fighting force.[21]

The primary tactic Westmoreland chose to accomplish his strategy of attrition came to be known as the search and destroy operation. These operations sent US infantry forces of multi-battalion strength and larger to find the main force NVA and NLF units, to fight them, and to inflict heavy casualties on them. If the strategy of attrition were to be successful, it was critical for the tactic of search and destroy operations to find and destroy the main force units of the NVA and the NLF.[22]

Westmoreland's strategy was not without its critics, though, and a number of them were some of the highest-ranking generals in the Marine Corps. Among these was Lieutenant General Victor Krulak, who proposed a different strategy. Krulak wanted to use an enclave military strategy for the war. This was a variation of an "oil-spot" strategy, which would occupy and pacify an area and then work outward to gradually control and pacify an increasingly larger area. He chose this strategy because as he studied Vietnam, Krulak saw that 80 percent of the people in South Vietnam lived in the fertile, coastal regions of the country where the majority of the country's rice crop was grown. These regions only extended inland for a few miles, and they only made up a small percentage of the country, but these coastal areas and the offshore waters produced large amounts of rice, salt, and fish. In contrast to the coastal regions, the interior of the country was not good for rice cultivation, and it had a small population. However, it was mountainous and much of it was covered with heavy vegetation, and this is where the NVA and the main force NLF battalions and regiments hid themselves.

Krulak knew much of the food supply for these units was obtained from the coastal regions of South Vietnam. If the enemy were denied this source of food, food could be brought down the trails from North Vietnam, but this would mean fewer military supplies could be brought to the fighters.[23]

So, there were basically two military strategies used by US ground forces in the Vietnam War. Westmoreland used the military strategy of attrition, and he primarily used the tactic of search and destroy missions to accomplish it. The other military strategy was the enclave strategy advocated by some of the leading generals of the US Marine Corps. For this strategy the Marine Corps used the CAP program as one of the central concepts.

This disagreement over strategy had a tremendous influence on the CAP program during the Vietnam War. The clash between the US Army and the US Marine Corps over strategy and tactics created an undercurrent of conflict which manifested itself in various, harmful ways during the war. In this conflict of opinions and practice the CAP program was often caught in the middle.

Also, the Government of the Republic of South Vietnam (GVN) played an important part in the story of the CAP program in the Vietnam War, and in the history of the entire US war in Vietnam. A good deal of the GVN was weak and ineffective. One reason for this was that there was a considerable amount of corruption in the GVN. It was difficult for the CAP program to convince the Vietnamese people they should be loyal to the central government when the GVN was corrupt and unresponsive to many of the people's needs. How to manage this problem was a primary question for the CAP program.

Looking at the CAP program as a counterinsurgency method will be valuable because this aspect of the history of the CAP program has been overlooked for the most part, and the CAP concept may have been a promising counterinsurgency technique in the Vietnam War. The historian John Prados said, "Almost all accounts of CAPs are either dry recitations in official Marine Corps official histories or close to the earth visions of single villages, and there has long been room for broader studies."[24] Evaluating the CAP program with counterinsurgency principles will also help determine whether the CAPs were an effective counterinsurgency concept in the Vietnam War. If they were, and if they were not used well, then this may point to an alternate strategy the United States could have used in Vietnam in which the CAPs would have played an integral part. The reverse needs to be considered, also. By using counterinsurgency principles to evaluate the performance of CAPs in Vietnam, it may be determined that the CAPs were not successful as a counterinsurgency concept in the Vietnam War. So, a study of CAPs within the framework of counterinsurgency principles will provide a better understanding of CAPs as a counterinsurgency concept in the Vietnam War, and a better understanding of how the CAPs were used in the war.

Chapter 1

Crisis and Response

In the early months of 1965, the situation in the Republic of Vietnam was going from bad to worse. A dizzying series of political coups had occurred during the previous year until some political stability appeared to have taken hold with the coming to power of Nguyen Van Thieu and Nguyen Cao Ky. This was small consolation, though, because the government's war against the NLF was progressing badly. Shortly after he took office, Ky said the situation was getting more difficult for the South Vietnamese forces: "In the Central Highlands … at least one regular North Vietnamese Army division had invaded this region. More troops had reinforced Vietcong units throughout the highlands with thousands of well-trained North Vietnamese regulars, including many leaders … the number of Vietcong incidents had increased dramatically. In short, the enemy was on the verge of cutting South Vietnam into two parts."[1]

The quality of the guerrilla forces and their increased aggressiveness were certainly factors in creating the crisis for South Victnam, but a primary rcason for thc crisis was how wcll thc guerrillas fought against the South Vietnamese Army (ARVN).

An example of this was the battle of Ap Bac fought in the Mekong Delta in January 1963. In this battle an ARVN force including mechanized troops and helicopter support attacked an inferior number of NLF fighters. Instead of retreating, the NLF force stood and fought the ARVN. The NLF unit defeated the ARVN troops and destroyed a number of helicopters and armored personnel carriers.[2] In the last days of December 1964, a major battle, which continued for four days, was fought close to the Vietnamese village of Binh Gia. In this fight, the enemy destroyed two battalions of ARVN troops and inflicted serious casualties on the relief force sent to help them.[3] The South Vietnamese were losing battle after battle to the enemy, and General William C. Westmoreland, commander of Military Assistance Command, Vietnam (MACV), sounded especially discouraged when he said, "The enemy was destroying battalions faster than they could be reconstituted and faster than we had planned to organize them under the ARVN's crash build-up plan."[4]

An enemy growing stronger and battlefield defeats might not have been critical if the ARVN had a strong sense of purpose and good morale. However, one significant sign of crumbling ARVN morale was a desertion rate of 5,000 to 7,000 men per month.[5] Some of these men may have simply gone to their villages to help with the crops, or to take care of family business, but the majority probably left to avoid the fighting. If matters were left to pursue their course, South Vietnam could soon lose the war, and it looked as if only more military help from the United States could prevent defeat.

Many South Vietnamese felt alienated from the ARVN because they saw it as an army originally formed by the French, and this may have been part of the reason for its poor morale and its poor performance. One Vietnamese scholar said, "ARVN had, as we say, a birth defect resulting from the difficulties and weaknesses inherent in the circumstances of its formation. It was a creation of the French colonial administration, set up and trained by the French."[6] This made it hard for the South Vietnamese to identify with ARVN as their army protecting their country, but the problem was aggravated because "ARVN's high-ranking soldiers were almost without exception products of French military academies or officers who rose within the ranks of the French expeditionary corps."[7] For many of the South Vietnamese people, and for many of the enlisted men who served in the ARVN, it was probably difficult to feel any great loyalty or pride for an army that appeared to be an extension of their colonial past.

While the situation in Vietnam deteriorated, in the United States, President Lyndon B. Johnson and his advisors were trying to find ways the United States could help prevent the South Vietnamese from being defeated by the insurgents. The defeat appeared to be imminent, and the solutions appeared to be few. US military assistance for the South Vietnamese was massive by this time. By the end of 1964 military advisers were serving down to battalion level with the South Vietnamese troops. In addition, MACV trained, equipped, and developed the South Vietnamese armed forces, and some combat support was supplied with US helicopters.[8] Still, the advisers, the equipment, and the training were not enough to avert the current crisis.

The position of most of the decision makers in the United States was that the NLF guerrilla organization in South Vietnam was created and controlled by North Vietnam.[9] They either did not understand or would not acknowledge the NLF was formed to a large degree as a response to the corruption and injustice of the GVN, and a nationalistic desire to unite the two Vietnams into one country.[10] It was thought that if North Vietnam would end its support of the guerrillas, the South Vietnamese could defeat the rebellion.

This thinking guided the US response when the US forces were attacked at the Pleiku base in the Central Highlands on February 7, 1965. Some of the US helicopter units supporting

South Vietnamese troops were stationed there, and Washington saw the attack as a message from the North Vietnamese to either stop US intervention in the war or suffer the consequences. Eight US servicemen were killed, and over one hundred were wounded. The attack also did extensive damage to the camp. The US saw it as a direct challenge from the North Vietnamese, and the US quickly struck back by sending aircraft to hit targets in North Vietnam.

Matters soon worsened with an NLF attack against US forces at Qui Nhon in South Vietnam on February 10, 1965, only three days after the attack at Pleiku. In this attack, twenty-three US soldiers were killed, and twenty-two were wounded. The United States responded with more bombing attacks on targets in North Vietnam. The Pentagon decided these air attacks on North Vietnam would continue, and concern for the protection of other US air facilities in South Vietnam grew because of the recent attacks on US bases.

The airbase at Danang was considered a prime target for the enemy because of the importance of the aircraft there in conducting the bombing attacks in North Vietnam, and the decision was made to land US Marines at Danang for the purpose of guarding the airbase. On March 8, 1965, US Marines began an amphibious landing in Danang harbor. The landing was unopposed, and many of the people there to greet them were young Vietnamese women who welcomed them with leis of flowers. Other Marines were flown into the Danang airbase, and over the next few days two Marine infantry battalions and some supporting units set up positions to guard the base. Their mission was clear: they were to defend the airbase and not to conduct offensive combat activities.

As the leaders in Washington decided what was to be done, and as the generals gave the troops orders, the Marines dug their defensive positions around the airbase at Danang. Philip Caputo was a lieutenant in this first group of Marines to arrive in Vietnam, and in his book, *A Rumor of War*, he wrote his impressions of the enlisted men in the platoon he commanded: "Most of them came from the ragged fringes of the Great American Dream, from city slums and dirt farms and Appalachian mining towns." He went on to say, though, the Marines gave these men "self-respect. A man who wore that uniform was somebody. He had passed a test few others could, He was not some down- on- his- luck loser pumping gas or washing cars for a dollar-fifty an hour, but somebody, a Marine."[11] They had gone through hard training, and they were told they were the best fighting men in the world. Most of them truly believed this, and many were proud to the point of arrogance. This was to be a great adventure, and they would have stories to tell.

The Marines worked, and they sat in their defensive positions and watched for the enemy. As they did this, they felt the intense heat of South Vietnam. The weather is always a consideration for people, but it is a greater concern for people who live outside. Caputo said, "Temperatures were irrelevant—the climate in Indochina does not lend itself to conventional standards of measurement." He continued to say, "the only valid measurement was what the heat could do to a man, and what it could do to him was simple enough: it could kill him, bake his brain, or wring the sweat out of him until he dropped from exhaustion."[12] While the Marines guarded the airbase, they endured the boredom of their assignment, and they endured the crushing heat of South Vietnam. They were ready for a fight, and many were eager at the prospect. They did not have long to wait.

The situation for ARVN forces was no less desperate because US Marines were guarding Danang, and the ARVN troops continued to be defeated by the NLF fighters. On April 1, 1965, President Johnson authorized the commitment of additional US troops to Vietnam, and he lifted some of the restrictions on their use in combat. This was not enough, though, in General Westmoreland's opinion. He thought the South Vietnamese were dangerously close to being defeated, and only the use of US troops to help them fight the NLF and the NVA could save South Vietnam.[13] In late July of 1965, Johnson approved Westmoreland's request for a large increase of US troops in South Vietnam. Also, Westmoreland received permission to use US combat troops to fight the enemy throughout South Vietnam. The gloves came off, and ground combat units of the United States were now fully committed to the fight in South Vietnam.

After they were given the mission of fighting the enemy the first months of combat were confusing for the Marines, and in many of the same ways combat continued to be confusing during the war. The men would go into the "bush" as it was called, on what were known as search and destroy operations. However, "There was no pattern to these patrols and operations. Without a front, flanks, or rear, we fought a formless war against a formless enemy who evaporated like the morning jungle mists, only to materialize in some unexpected place."[14] In this confused situation, death could come at any time, and from any direction. There might be a single shot from a sniper, or a number of shots would shatter the heavy heat. Or, mortar rounds would explode close to or among the men. Even the ground the Marines walked on was not safe. A man could be walking and suddenly be consumed by the blast of a booby trap he had stepped on. The guerrillas would not stand and fight; they hit and ran. The Marines were confused, and they were angry.

To add further to the combustible nature of this confusing situation, Caputo said the Marines were told in a briefing to be careful not to shoot civilians. If a Vietnamese was armed, he or she was a guerrilla. However, if a Vietnamese ran, this was also a guerrilla, and could be killed. It was suggested that the Vietnamese might be a civilian running because he was scared. Finally, the officer said those in higher command had said that as far as they were concerned, any dead Vietnamese was a dead guerrilla.[15] The Marines rarely saw the guerrillas but they often saw civilians, and often some of the civilians could be guerrilla fighters. The Marines did not know with any certainty who was a guerrilla and who was a friend. The potential for indiscriminate mistakes was great.

Search and Destroy

From the time he was a cadet at West Point, William C. Westmoreland had showed strong leadership ability, and he continued to demonstrate this ability throughout most of his career. After commanding artillery units in combat in World War II, he went on to lead a regiment of paratroopers in the Korean War. In these capacities he served with distinction, and he later commanded the elite 101st Airborne Division. Problems were mounting in South Vietnam in the early 1960s and the US needed a strong leader to head the military assistance program for South Vietnam. With his distinguished record Westmoreland appeared to be an excellent choice for the position, and he was placed in command.

Westmoreland studied the military theory of the NLF and the NVA, and he closely watched how the guerrillas were fighting the South Vietnamese. He saw them using the concepts of revolutionary war Mao Zedong developed to win the Chinese Civil War. Basically, Westmoreland saw three phases in revolutionary warfare. In the first phase, the guerrillas were on the defensive. They tried to gain control of the population, and they conducted small guerrilla actions against the government. As their strength grew, they moved into the second phase, and regular combat units were formed, the pace of attacks increased, and the regular combat units attacked government forces. In the third phase, the guerrillas greatly increased their strength, and large guerrilla units went on the offensive to defeat the government's forces and to take complete control of the country. In early 1965,

Westmoreland saw that the enemy was forming into larger regimental and division sized units, and they were attacking and defeating South Vietnamese forces with bold and frequent attacks. He thought the enemy was moving into the third phase of revolutionary warfare, and he concluded strong action needed to be taken quickly.[16]

There were three phases to the plan Westmoreland conceived to fight the war. In the first phase US troops would protect the large logistical bases being constructed for the influx of more troops. If a large concentration of NLF or NVA troops was discovered, or if opposing forces presented a threat, US troops could be quickly sent to fight them. In the second phase, US forces would take the initiative and attack and eliminate guerrilla base camps. Going after the base camps could also force the large units of the NLF and the NVA to fight, and this would give US forces the opportunity to destroy them with superior firepower. The third phase would be combat with the remaining large units, and here the large NLF and NVA units would be destroyed or driven from the country and blocked from returning to South Vietnam. While US troops were accomplishing this, the ARVN would be working primarily on pacification among the people of South Vietnam. Westmoreland said the ARVN had "greater compatibility" with the people than the Americans did, and he thought they would be better suited for the pacification role.[17]

The strategy Westmoreland chose for the war was one of attrition. This meant he intended to have US forces kill so many of the NLF and NVA soldiers that eventually the enemy would not have enough soldiers to replace those who were killed. Evidence of the success of this strategy would be the reaching of the "crossover" point where more NLF and NVA soldiers were being killed than were either being recruited to the NLF in South Vietnam or were being sent into South Vietnam from North Vietnam. Westmoreland's thinking was that North Vietnam and the NLF had a limited source of manpower, and this supply of manpower would be further lessened as the ARVN pacified more of South Vietnam and restricted NLF access to potential recruits in the pacified areas. Because US government policy limited him to fighting the war within South Vietnam, Westmoreland said he saw no acceptable alternative to using a strategy of attrition to fight the war.[18]

There were other strategies proposed by respected military figures, but Westmoreland chose a strategy of attrition. A strategy of attrition is brutal, and the violence inherent in it is immense. The war in Vietnam was going to be fundamentally a counterinsurgency war, and much of the war would be fought in populated areas. Because of this the potential for high numbers of civilian deaths was great. Much of the loss of life among the civilians of Vietnam during the war can arguably be traced to Westmoreland's decision to use a strategy of attrition.

The basic tactic to accomplish the attrition strategy of Westmoreland's plan for the war was to have US battalions and regiments pursuing and engaging the battalions and the regiments of the NLF and the NVA. These were the search and destroy missions.[19] When US troops first began fighting in South Vietnam, this approach may have had some merit because large guerrilla units were running rampant throughout the country as they inflicted a series of defeats on the South Vietnamese forces, and the confidence and the momentum of the guerrillas had to be broken. Only US forces of at least battalion strength would stand a chance of defeating these units in pitched battles. Also, US troops needed to show the enemy they could beat them in a fight, and they needed to show the enemy they were in South Vietnam to defeat them. Westmoreland counted on the mobility that helicopters gave US infantry to out-maneuver guerrilla forces in combat, and he also thought the US forces could crush them with artillery and air power when the enemy was locked in battle with the infantry.

This was the sort of war the US military usually waged in the past, and it did it well. As the historian Russell F. Weigley said, Westmoreland believed in, "carrying the war to the enemy, and at winning victory by the means sanctioned by the most deeply rooted historical American conceptions of strategy, the destruction of the enemy's armed forces and of his ability to wage war."[20] How long using large US infantry units to seek out NLF and NVA forces should have remained the principal focus of US actions is an important question, though. As time passed, fewer of these operations made contact with the opposing forces. Still, Westmoreland persisted with his chosen course of action.

The use of search and destroy tactics in the first part of the war had mixed results. An early battle perceived as a success for search and destroy tactics was the battle of the Ia Drang valley in November 1965. This battle took place after a series of sweeps succeeded in locating a large unit of the NVA, which decided to stand and fight the Americans. The battle ended with over 1,200 NVA soldiers being killed. However, over three hundred US. soldiers also died in the fighting.[21] Some of these early search and destroy operations found the enemy, but many did not. One of the first US Army units sent to Vietnam was the 173rd Airborne Brigade commanded by Brigadier General Ellis Williamson. After his unit conducted some of these operations, Williamson sounded disgusted with the tactic when he said, "I hope that we have conducted our last 'search and destroy' operation. I am thoroughly convinced that running into the jungle with a lot of people without a fixed target is a lot of effort, a lot of physical energy expended. A major portion of our effort evaporates into the air."[22]

One reason operations were not usually finding the guerrillas was that they were based on poor intelligence. This was a problem that persisted, and later in the war US Army General Fred Weyand showed his frustration with the problem, "In South Vietnam, the sole basis for effective, meaningful operations is specific intelligence information." He went on to say, "without it, the commander is left groping almost aimlessly."[23]

The US troops used for the search and destroy sweeps might have been used more effectively in other ways, such as small-unit patrolling and pacification efforts. Of course, the NLF and the NVA were able to adjust their responses in these situations, and how they reacted to the search and destroy tactics was important to the success of the tactics.

When US troops entered the war, the NVA and the NLF confronted an unfamiliar enemy, and they knew they would have to develop tactics to use against the immense power of the US military. However, the NLF and the NVA had an advantage when they started fighting US troops because many of their officers and non-commissioned officers previously fought the French in the French-Indochinese War, and some of the NLF soldiers had been fighting the ARVN for quite some time. Both the French and the ARVN often used tactics similar to the search and destroy operations of the Americans, so the NLF and the NVA already had a number of proven tactics to use against the US.

The primary problem the NLF and the NVA faced was how to deal with the helicopter mobility and the massive firepower of the Americans. In the Ia Drang Valley battle the NVA saw how the US troops fought, and the lessons they drew from the battle were distributed to all of the NVA troop commanders. US helicopter mobility was swift and US firepower was tremendous, but the NVA saw weaknesses in the way the Americans used these strengths. The Americans usually strafed and bombed an area before helicopters landed troops, and as a result of this the Americans lost the element of surprise. Because of this, any NVA troops in the area could quickly move to evade the bombing and the following infantry assault from the helicopters.

Two of the key tactics the NVA decided to use against US troops after the Ia Drang Valley battle were based on close-quarter fighting and surprise. In a battle the NVA wanted to get as close to the US infantry as they could, so the Americans would be hesitant to use artillery and air support because it might hit their own troops. The NVA commanders were also told to watch the patterns of activity and movement of the Americans during the search and destroy operations, and to see how the Americans reacted to NVA sniper fire and attacks while they were on these operations. Using this information, the NVA would create diversions to lead the US troops into areas where carefully planned ambushes were prepared. If an ambush was successful, the NVA forces could also have additional ambushes prepared along roads or in landing zones the Americans would be likely to use to bring reinforcements to the ambushed American unit. In all situations where they fought the Americans, the NVA commanders were instructed to make the fight as lethal as possible in a very short period of time. After the fight was ended, the NVA troops would quickly leave the area. In this way the NVA attempted to inflict heavy casualties on US forces while avoiding the punishing power of American artillery and airstrikes which would inevitably be called in to support the ambushed US troops.[24]

Participating in the search and destroy operations was physically trying and mentally and emotionally confusing for the US infantrymen. In many ways these operations were as physically demanding, or worse, than some of the Pacific island campaigns of World War II such as Guadalcanal and Okinawa. The heat and the humidity were crushing, and during the monsoon season it sometimes rained continuously for weeks on end. As the men walked through and lived in the jungles and the forests of Vietnam, leeches, parasites, funguses, malaria, and dysentery were common problems. Through all of this they carried heavy loads of weapons and ammunition in case they had to fight the guerrillas. Even when they did not find the enemy, the infantrymen were routinely subjected to the dangers of sniper fire, booby traps, and mortar attacks which often killed and wounded men. A Marine infantryman said he thought they walked around as if they were in a fog, because they had little idea what they were trying to accomplish on many of the operations. Their primary interest was to save their own lives and the lives of their fellow Marines. As far as the Vietnamese civilians they encountered were concerned, he said the Marines were indifferent or hostile toward them, and they made few efforts to win the "hearts and minds" of the people.[25]

Considering the circumstances of the search and destroy missions, it is easy to understand how some men began to think and act this way. Often the infantry units were sent into areas on sweeps to see if the guerrillas would initiate a fight. So, in effect, the US units were bait. In these cases the guerrillas had the initiative, and they fought from prepared positions in areas they chose.[26] Still, US commanders placed their faith in the idea that when the guerrillas fought US troops the weight of US firepower could be brought to bear on them, and killing the NLF and NVA soldiers would win the war of attrition.

Another Way to Fight the War

General Westmoreland chose the strategy of attrition and the tactic of search and destroy operations for the war in Vietnam, but within the United States Marine Corps there was significant disagreement with this approach. Some of the key US Marine Corps generals responsible for planning and fighting the war thought a more classic counterinsurgency strategy would be appropriate in Vietnam. Part of the reason for this may have been the influence fighting counterinsurgency campaigns in the Caribbean during the early part of the twentieth century had on the institutional memory of the Marine Corps. Major General Lewis W. Walt became the commanding general of the III Marine Amphibious Force in Vietnam, and he said he learned his skills as a junior officer, "from men who had fought Sandino in Nicaragua or Charlemagne in Haiti."[27]

The lessons of counterinsurgency warfare in the Caribbean related to young Marine officers may have been formative to some degree, but their influence should be qualified. Both Marine Commandant General Wallace M. Greene and Lieutenant General Victor H. Krulak were in favor of an approach to the war which placed more emphasis on counterinsurgency. They wanted a counterinsurgency strategy which placed more emphasis on pacification in Vietnam, and US Army General Maxwell Taylor and US Army General James Gavin also agreed with this assessment.[28] So, the choice of a strategy more in keeping with this counterinsurgency theory may also have been the result of a professional military evaluation of the problem, as well as being influenced by the experiences of the Marine Corps in the Caribbean wars.

Among the Marine Corps generals, Krulak was one of the most vocal, and arguably one of the most abrasive, proponents of an alternative strategy in Vietnam. After graduating from Annapolis Naval Academy, Krulak became a Marine Corps officer and served with distinction during World War II. He was a decorated combat veteran, and he was also an officer of intellect and vision. An important part he played in the war was in the development of the landing crafts necessary for amphibious landings.[29] Also, in 1946, Krulak began working on the revolutionary concept of using helicopters to carry troops into combat.[30] His work helped to create the helicopter assault concept for the Marine Corps and for the US Army.

As the possibility of the United States having to fight against guerrilla movements in the future became more of a probability, Krulak closely studied insurgency and counterinsurgency warfare. In 1962 he was chosen as Special Assistant for Counter-Insurgency and Special Activities, and in this capacity, he reported directly to Secretary of Defense Robert McNamara and he also met on a regular basis with President John F. Kennedy.[31] Kennedy studied insurgency warfare, and he saw insurgency warfare as a serious challenge for the US. Partly because of this the insurgency in the Republic of Vietnam became a central focus of Washington's attention. Krulak went to Vietnam eight times between 1962 and 1964 in an effort to find how the US could help the Republic of Vietnam win the guerrilla war being fought there. During these visits Krulak increased his understanding of the problems the South Vietnamese were facing, and the problems inherent to a counterinsurgency war.

On several occasions Krulak met with Sir Robert Thompson, who played an important part in helping the British win a counterinsurgency war in Malaya, and Krulak was impressed with some basic principles of counterinsurgency Thompson discussed with him. Thompson told Krulak, "The people's trust is primary. It will come hard because they are fearful and suspicious. Protection is the most important thing you can bring them. After that comes health. And, after that, many things—land, prosperity, education, and privacy to name a few." Krulak became convinced that a complete understanding and practice of these ideas was necessary if the counterinsurgency war were to be won in South Vietnam.[32]

In 1964 as the commitment of US troops to the ground war in Vietnam was approaching, Krulak was designated the Commanding General, Fleet Marine Force, Pacific. In this position he was responsible for the training, equipping, and supplying of all the Marines in the Pacific, but he had no operational control over them in Vietnam when the war started. Because he anticipated the United States would probably soon be fighting in South Vietnam, Krulak implemented a rigorous training program for the Marines that included many of the lessons he had learned about counterinsurgency warfare.[33] Once the war began Krulak was very vocal in his opinions of how the war should be conducted.

Krulak disagreed with Westmoreland's attrition strategy, and in June of 1965 he developed a comprehensive, alternative strategic approach that reflected his knowledge of counterinsurgency warfare, the NLF and the NVA, and Vietnam. The goal to be attained in Vietnam was not the territory of the country, he thought; it was the wealth of the country and the control and the loyalty of the population. He saw that two-thirds of the population and approximately three-fourths of the rice production in South Vietnam were in the coastal regions of the country and in the Mekong Delta. The essence of his concept was that if these areas were controlled by the ARVN and their allies the NLF would be cut off from the food, the recruits, and the sources of intelligence among the people which are vital for the continuation of an insurgency.[34]

Krulak proposed an enclave strategy to separate the majority of the people and the majority of the wealth of South Vietnam from the guerrillas. This was a classic "oil-spot" counterinsurgency strategy, which would clear the guerrillas from an area, and then progressively clear them from areas adjacent to the cleared area. Along the coastal region of northern South Vietnam, the Marines had established three enclaves at Chu Lai, Danang, and Phu Bai, and Krulak said these would be the initial enclaves which would expand and then merge together along the coast of South Vietnam. To merge the enclave areas, US forces and their allies would conduct operations to clear the guerrillas from the areas adjacent to the enclaves until the enclaves controlled the population and the rich agricultural regions of the coastal region. Krulak thought if this were done, and if similar efforts gained control of the Mekong Delta, the guerrillas would be forced back into the less populated areas of the interior. In these interior areas a smaller civilian population would mean US forces could more easily detect the movements of the guerrilla soldiers. Also, in the less-populated areas, there would be fewer potential recruits available for the guerrillas, less food for their soldiers, and less intelligence information available from the population about allied forces.[35]

Krulak also thought the guerrillas had one basic tactic, and they used that one tactic to defeat the French and to inflict many defeats on the South Vietnamese forces. The NLF and NVA forces chose an isolated position and then carefully developed a plan of attack. As they prepared the attack, they located the likely routes of approach relief forces would take to rescue the attacked position, and along these routes they placed ambushes for the relief forces. In the fight the damage done to the attacked position was important, but the attack on the more vulnerable relief columns was calculated to do the most damage.[36]

This was the tactic the guerrillas used to attack fixed positions, but Krulak knew they also used a variation of this tactic to lure search and destroy forces into prepared ambushes where the relief forces sent to support the attacked unit could be ambushed. His proposed solution was to eliminate isolated positions with their vulnerable lines of support and supply and to keep fixed positions within the enclaves. Instead of using search and destroy operations he wanted an aggressive practice of continuous patrolling and ambushes outside the enclave areas to disrupt the guerrillas and to discover any concentrations of their forces. When guerrilla concentrations were discovered, attacks on them could be made based on sound intelligence. In addition, operations would be conducted to clear the guerrillas from areas adjacent to the enclave areas in order to expand the enclaves.[37]

In Krulak's opinion, his proposed enclave plan would take the initiative from the guerrillas by denying them the opportunity to use the one tactic which was so successful for them in the past. If the guerrillas were denied access to the food and the people of the coastal region, the NLF and the NVA would have to attack the defenses of the enclaves. Here the US forces would have the benefit of prepared defensive positions and US air and artillery support. The guerrillas also might attempt to attack communication between the enclaves, but surveillance in those areas would be extensive, and it would not be easy for the guerrilla forces to conduct the planned ambushes they favored. Also, relief forces and air and artillery support from the enclaves could attack them.

The enclave strategy was intended to lessen many of the guerrillas' strengths and to capitalize on the strengths of the allied forces. For the NLF and the NVA to be successful, it was critical for them to have access to the people. Among the people they could get the food, the recruits, and the intelligence necessary for the insurgency to succeed. Without intelligence they were blind, without recruits they had no soldiers, and without food they would starve. To defeat the guerillas Krulak proposed a classic counterinsurgency enclave strategy which would take away the guerrillas' strength and maximize the strengths of the allied forces.[38]

Krulak was convinced his strategic approach to the war based on an oil-spot concept of pacification was the correct strategy to use in Vietnam, and he made his thinking known to General Westmoreland. In a discussion of this alternative strategy, Westmoreland told Krulak he thought the oil-spot strategy Krulak proposed was good, but he said it would take too much time. Of course, by saying this Westmoreland was implying the strategy of attrition and the tactics of search and destroy missions could win the war more quickly. In his typically blunt manner, Krulak got to the heart of the matter when he responded, "I suggested to him that we didn't have time to do it any other way." Krulak criticized the use of search and destroy tactics directly when he continued, "if we left the people to the enemy, glorious victories in the hinterland would be little more than blows in the air—and we would end up losing the war."[39]

Krulak's frustration with the situation in Vietnam seems to have been growing, and in November of 1965 he wrote to

Secretary of Defense Robert McNamara telling him the war in the highly populated regions of South Vietnam was being fought over the minds of the people, and to win this war the guerrillas had to first be kept away from the people. He said after a security shield was placed between the people and the guerrillas, the NLF political infrastructure could be eliminated within the cleared area. McNamara's reply to Krulak was similar to Westmoreland's; he said the idea had merit, but it would take too long.[40]

Chapter 2

An Enclave Strategy and Joint Action Platoons in I Corps

In June of 1965, Marine Corps Major General Lewis W. Walt took command of the III Marine Amphibious Force (III MAF) which was responsible for I Corps, comprised of the five northernmost provinces in South Vietnam. Walt served in combat in the Pacific with a Marine Raider Battalion in World War II. These were specialized units trained for guerrilla warfare behind Japanese lines, and this experience may have increased Walt's understanding of insurgency warfare. During the war Walt served with distinction, and he received a number of decorations for his heroism. Walt then served in the Korean War before his later assignment in South Vietnam. Walt agreed with the enclave strategy Krulak proposed, and when he evaluated the situation in Vietnam after he assumed command of the III MAF he became even more convinced an approach more oriented to an enclave strategy was necessary.[1]

General Westmoreland was the commander of all the US military forces in South Vietnam, but Walt was allowed some freedom of interpretation in his actions becausc hc was a senior regional commander. Rather than giving Walt direct orders,

Westmoreland gave him broader missions to accomplish. Walt was then able to use his own judgment as to how to accomplish the missions. As a result of this, Walt was able to pursue the enclave strategy he favored in I Corps, to some extent.[2]

The plan Walt intended to implement for the three Marine bases of Chu Lai, Danang, and Phu Bai was similar in concept to the enclave strategy Krulak presented for the war. He wanted to establish a main line of heavily constructed bunkers capable of supporting each other as the main defensive line for each base. In the event of a major guerrilla attack, the Marines could fight off the attack from these positions. Beyond this line a line of manned outpost positions would be established from which a mobile defense would be conducted. He stressed that constant patrolling throughout the area should be maintained to prevent the guerrillas from concentrating forces, to gather intelligence, and to give advanced warning of potential attacks on the base defenses. Small reconnaissance patrols would also be sent far beyond the perimeters of the enclaves into areas which had been areas of safety for the guerrillas. When the patrols found guerrilla camps or movement, they could call for air strikes or artillery attacks. This would keep the guerrilla fighters off balance in areas which were previously safe havens, and because of this it would show them they were not the only hunters in the war; they were now the hunted.[3]

While the plans for the base defenses were being put into place, the Marines innovated to find ways the local South Vietnamese forces could help the Marines defend the enclaves. In the Chu Lai area, joint patrols of local South Vietnamese defense forces and Marines patrolled through the area, and the Marines brought PF units to their camps for training. In the Danang region, South Vietnamese Regional Forces (RFs) and Marine units coordinated their various military operations. Also, on patrols and operations in the Danang area, Marines used PF militiamen as interpreters and guides.[4] Altogether, these measures worked to add to the defense of the Marine enclaves by capitalizing on the strengths of both the South Vietnamese forces and the Marines.

Pacification was a critical part of the enclave strategy the Marines were practicing in the I Corps area, and the Marines were trying different ideas in an effort to find methods that would work. In one of the first instances, the Marines thought by occupying the Vietnamese village of Le My close to the Danang perimeter defensive line they could improve the airbase defenses. Some of the first patrols in the area of the village encountered sniper fire, and a battalion operation was conducted to drive the enemy from the village. When the NLF fighters were driven out of Le My, the Marines secured the village and questioned the men they found there. Later a few of the men were sent to Danang for further questioning. After a few days, South Vietnamese RFs and PFs took over security duties in Le My and the Marines moved into a defensive perimeter position around the village. The South Vietnamese forces then did further screening of the people in the village in an effort to eliminate any remaining guerrilla elements. Shortly after this, the Marines helped the people build medical dispensaries, schools, bridges, and a marketplace in Le My. To improve the protection of Le My, the Marines trained the PFs and helped them set up defensive positions.[5]

In this attempt the Marines gave a partial definition of their idea of pacification when their civil affairs officer said their intent was "to create an administration, supported by the people, and capable of leading, treating, feeding, and protecting themselves by the time the battalion was moved to another area of operations."[6] Success in Le My was important for the Marines' goal of pacifying the Vietnamese villages. However, this was one of the first Marine pacification projects, and initially it appeared to work well enough so that it became a model for future Marine efforts.[7]

Even though the pacification of Le My seemed to have gone well, there were still some problems. When Krulak visited the village, he spoke with the district chief who was happy with the improvements the Marines had helped make possible. The district chief showed Krulak the schools and the dispensaries, and then he asked Krulak if the Marines would stay. Krulak told him Marines would be close to the village, and they would help the people if the NLF fighters returned. In the meantime the PFs would be in charge of security for Le My. The district chief was not happy with this response.[8] In his discussions with Krulak, Robert Thompson stressed to Krulak the importance of protection for the people in counterinsurgency pacification operations, and Krulak agreed with Thompson's advice. The pacification of Le My gave the people of the village access to dispensaries for their health and schools for their education, but all of this would mean nothing if the guerrillas could return and kill them for cooperating with the Americans.

> One of the biggest problems for the people of Vietnam at this time was a lack of good medical care. Soon after they arrived, the Marines began setting up medical dispensaries for the Vietnamese, and this program of medical care spread quickly throughout the three Marine enclaves of Chu Lai, Danang, and Phu Bai. At first some of the Vietnamese were suspicious of the program, but eventually the services of the dispensaries became popular, and dental care was also provided. In the more remote and less safe areas, a Marine patrol would accompany a Navy corpsman (medic) to a village where the patrol would guard the area while the corpsman helped the Vietnamese with minor medical problems.[9] This program of medical care for the Vietnamese people eventually became one of the most popular pacification services the Americans provided during the Vietnam War.

A key part of the enclave plan was the denial of rice to the guerrillas, and the Marines started operations to do this in the Danang area as they expanded their Tactical Area of Responsibility (TAOR) into a densely populated region south of Danang. The Marine commander asked a number of Vietnamese village chiefs in the new area to give their support to the Marines. Initially the village chiefs were uncertain, but after the Marines defeated the local NLF forces in a battle, the chiefs became more confident the Marines could protect them. One of them approached the battalion commander of the Marines and told him the NLF forces were coming into the area, as they did each year, to take what they considered to be their portion of the rice which was soon to be harvested. The village chiefs wanted to know if the Marines would protect the villagers so they could keep all of the rice they harvested. The Marine commander agreed to this, and the Marines set up a protective screen of troops around the rice harvest. The NLF staged an attack on the Marines, but it was defeated, and the operation was successful.

During this period, other Marine units in the Danang and Chu Lai regions protected rice harvests, and the NLF was kept from taking a large amount of rice needed to feed its soldiers. This protection of the rice harvests, called Golden Fleece, was so successful, and it was so popular with the Vietnamese farmers, that a similar operation was scheduled to protect the next rice harvest.[10]

The Marines continued to increase the size of the enclaves they occupied, but one of their most crucial jobs was to clear the NLF from the villages within the enclaves. If hidden NLF members remained in the villages, the villagers would not feel safe in cooperating with the Marines because of the threat of reprisal. In an effort to root out NLF agents in the villages, the Marines used the classic counterinsurgency tactic of "cordon and search" in which a force of Marines surrounded a village, and ARVN troops entered thc villagc and gathered all of the people together to check their government identification cards. As this was being done the village was searched for hidden weapons and for people who were trying to hide. Also, the Marines made medical assistance available for the people, and the people of the village were usually fed. These operations became known as County Fairs, and their use in getting rid of the NLF presence in Vietnamese villages was considered to be successful. Because of this the Marines continued to use them with varying degrees of success.[11]

Many of the pacification projects of the Marines showed promise, but the counterinsurgency necessity of protecting the people from the guerrillas was a recurring problem when South Vietnamese militia forces were used to defend the villages. When the Marines expanded the Danang enclave area, they encouraged the ARVN to develop a pacification plan for a number of villages close to Danang. The area where the villages were located was behind the protective screen of the Marines' expansion from Danang, but civic action activities and a military presence in the villages were needed to keep the NLF from infiltrating into the area to influence and intimidate the people.

According to the plan, RF and PF troops were stationed in the villages and Marines were close enough to some of the villages to help protect them from NLF attack. The control of the people was important for the NLF also, and they fought back when the RF and PF forces were stationed in the villages. The NLF forces targeted the villages defended by thc RF and PF units, and they stayed away from the areas where there was Marine protection. One after another, most of the RF- and PF-defended villages were attacked by the NLF, and the defending forces were defeated. Eventually, the plan to expand the pacified area through the use of South Vietnamese militia forces had to be halted for a period of time. The glaring problem was that the South Vietnamese militia units were neither trained well enough nor equipped well enough to fight and defeat the NLF.[12]

The Marines also had problems performing civic action and defense duties in the villages they attempted to pacify. They were not able to spend much time defending the villages and helping with more time-consuming civic action projects, because the infantry units were needed for combat missions. In some instances, the pacified villages were close to the Marine camps, but they were not close enough to keep the villages from being vulnerable to NLF infiltration. On various occasions village officials in the supposedly pacified villages were assassinated by the NLF, and in Le My, where one of the first pacification operations took place, a village official was buried alive after he was tortured by the NLF.[13] These hard lessons showed that protection of the people was the most important part of counterinsurgency, and without it there could be no pacification.

On one of his trips to Vietnam, General Krulak observed the County Fair cordon and search operations, and he saw some significant problems with them. The idea was a good counterinsurgency technique, in his opinion, but it was being executed poorly in some respects. While the Marines guarded a perimeter around the village, ARVN troops searched the village and checked the identification cards of the villagers. Krulak thought the ARVN did a poor job of this, and he thought the ARVN did not like working with the Vietnamese people. Another problem he saw was the lack of a permanent security presence in the village after the Marines and the ARVN left. NLF forces could easily return because there was no security force left behind to protect the village.[14]

Krulak's observations brought him to the conclusion that the Marines could not depend on the ARVN to do some of the pacification duties, at least without improvements in the ARVN, and until the ARVN did improve their performance the Marines would have to perform the pacification duties themselves. Also, Krulak's observations and the experience of the pacification program were underscoring the fact that a lack of security in the villages to be pacified was a central problem for the pacification program at this time.

The Joint Action Platoons

The United States Marine Corps established three enclaves in the northern coastal region of South Vietnam, and the northernmost of these was Phu Bai. The Third Battalion of the Fourth Marine Regiment (3/4) was responsible for the security of the enclave and airbase at Phu Bai. The TAOR continued to be increased for 3/4, and this was straining the abilities of the regiment to adequately defend the base. The aircraft at the airbase were high-priority targets for the NLF, and the regimental staff became concerned about attacks from Vietnamese hamlets located close to the camp. Captain John Mullen was the Civil Affairs officer for the regiment, and he proposed a possible solution for the problem to Lieutenant Colonel William Taylor, the regimental commander. Mullen knew the South Vietnamese military had militia units at the regional and the local levels. The regional militias were the RFs, and the local militias were the PFs. Technically these troops were under the control of the South Vietnamese Army, but in fact the province chiefs controlled the Regional Forces, and the village or district chiefs controlled the Popular Forces. Mullen suggested to the regimental commander that the Popular Forces in the villages around the base could be organized to help in the defense of Phu Bai.[15]

The decision to request the use of the South Vietnamese Popular Forces in the defense of the camp may have indicated how concerned the Marine commander was about the security of Phu Bai. The military effectiveness of South Vietnamese troops was generally held in low regard by the Americans, and the Popular Forces were among the least respected of all the South Vietnamese military units. Generally, they were poorly trained, poorly equipped, poorly led, and poorly paid. One of the few benefits for a member of the Popular Forces was that he could serve close to his home. Regardless, Colonel Taylor requested the use of some Popular Forces, and he was given a limited degree of control over six Popular Forces platoons. Shortly after this, Cullen C. Zimmerman, the executive officer of 3/4, drew up plans to create a unit made up of Marines and PF militia.[16]

The choice of the man to lead the new unit was fortunate. In June of 1965 Lieutenant Paul R. Ek was serving on the staff of the Third Marine Regiment at Danang as a liaison officer to the South Vietnamese. When he was asked to take this special assignment, he accepted it and reported to Lt. Colonel Taylor at Phu Bai in July. Ek's credentials for the job were impressive. On Okinawa he had attended an intensive Vietnamese language course, and as a result of this he spoke Vietnamese well. Also, prior to his serving on the staff of the Third Marine Regiment he served as an advisor to the Vietnamese Special Forces.[17] His language ability and his experience with the Vietnamese Special Forces made Ek a natural choice to form the new unit of Popular Forces and Marines.

When Ek reported to Phu Bai, Taylor told him the TAOR at Phu Bai had been expanded, and Taylor was concerned that he did not have enough men available to provide adequate defense for the expanded area. Taylor instructed Ek to formulate a plan to use Marines and Popular Forces in a combined unit for defense of the Phu Bai area.

The operational concept Ek conceived for the use of the Popular Forces with the Marines drew generally on his knowledge of counterinsurgency warfare, and particularly on his understanding of the infrastructure organization (the political and economic framework) of the NLF. In the villages Ek intended to have the PFs and the Marines build their own infrastructure to win the loyalty of the people by giving assistance to them. In this respect he said his method differed from the NLF's use of terror to gain a sort of loyalty from the people based on fear.

As the Marines and the PFs created their own infrastructure in the villages, they would be destroying the village infrastructure of the NLF. To do this there were several fundamental duties Ek set for the members of the unit. They had to provide protection for the people and for the village, and they had to gather intelligence information. They also had to conduct psychological warfare work and gain the good will of the people in the villages. These duties were the spokes of the plan Ek developed, and he saw the hub of the wheel in his plan as the training of the Marines and the Popular Forces militiamen.[18]

> Ek was told to combine four Marine rifle squads with four Popular Forces platoons to create a Joint Action Company (JAC). Each of the Marine squads was made up of three fire teams of four men each with a corporal as the fire team leader. There was a sergeant as the squad leader, and an assistant squad leader who was armed with an M-79 grenade launcher. Because of the specialized nature of the work, a US Navy corpsman (medic) was assigned to each of the Marine squads. Each of the fifteen-man Marine squads was combined with a Popular Forces platoon of between thirty and forty men. The PF platoon was commanded by a sergeant, and the other men in the platoon were all privates. The headquarters for the JAC was made up of Ek as the company commander, an ARVN lieutenant as the liaison officer, and three PFs for Vietnamese radio communication.[19]

Altogether, Ek's plan for the platoons looked impressive in these initial phases. A combined force of Popular Forces and Marines working at the village level to provide civic action and protection for the people could be a valuable part of a counterinsurgency war in South Vietnam. Regardless of how good the plan looked, though, its success or failure would depend on how well the Marines interacted with the Popular Forces and the people of the villages. Because of this, how the Marines were chosen and prepared for the new assignment was critical.

The Marines for the JAC company were carefully chosen, and Ek trained them himself before they joined the PFs to form the new unit. Volunteers from the infantry units were requested, and after Ek interviewed them he chose the volunteers he thought were motivated to live and work with the PFs. In addition, he wanted Marines who had already been in combat, and who could think and act quickly in unusual situations. After Ek chose the Marines, he trained them for a week to prepare them for their new job. In the training Ek taught the Marines Vietnamese customs, and he also taught them how the new unit would interact with the Vietnamese political and military organizations in the rural area where they would operate. An important part of the training was teaching the men how to perform intelligence activities in the villages. Also, Ek taught the men the tactics of the NLF. Ek's purpose was to make them capable of being accepted by the villagers as a part of the community while the Marines accomplished their military duties.[20]

Because the Joint Action Company combined the Popular Forces militia and the Marines in one unit, the command structure was unique. Partly because it could look similar to a colonial relationship, during the Vietnam War the South Vietnamese were adamantly opposed to the encadrement of US troops with South Vietnamese troops. The Joint Action Companies were the only units in the war which combined South Vietnamese and US troops in a unit in which the leader of the US troops was usually in command.[21] The sensitivity to the question was reflected in the intricate command structure of the newly established unit.

> The administrative authority and the military operational authority were divided at both the district and the village level. The Vietnamese district chief had administrative

responsibility for the Popular Forces in his district, and the Marine battalion commander had military operational control in the district. At the village level where the combined platoons worked, the Vietnamese village chief controlled the civil administration of the village while the combined platoons were responsible for the military security of the villages. The Marine squad leader commanded the platoon, and the sergeant commanding the Popular Forces in the platoon became his assistant; each squad in the platoon had a Marine fire team of four men and a squad of approximately ten PFs. The Marines in the squads were the designated leaders, but they also had counterparts who were Vietnamese, and for military operations the Marines led the squads and the platoons, Ek said. This was a maze of authority and personalities, and whether or not the platoons could work successfully in the villages depended to a great extent on the way the Marines interacted with the South Vietnamese.

After the Marine and PF personnel were assigned to their platoons, classes were given to share the strengths of each group with the other group. The Marines taught their tactics and their discipline to the PFs, as well as methods of civilian population control. For their part, the PFs taught the Marines Vietnamese customs, Vietnamese language, the terrain of the village area, and information about the NLF in the area. The training did not end with the classes, though. The Marines and the PFs continued to learn from each other and to teach each other as they lived and worked together.[22]

The Marines may have taught the Popular Forces some important skills, but they also learned a great deal from the PFs. A Marine who served with a combined platoon later in the war said many of the members of the Popular Forces were experienced veterans who learned combat skills fighting a guerrilla war for years, and this was especially true of some of the older

PFs who had fought either the French or the Viet Minh during the French Indochinese War. This Marine said the Marines taught the PFs some of the technical features of their newer weaponry, but often, "they showed us stuff that we didn't know." As an example of this, he said, the PFs taught the Marines different techniques of using booby traps and other explosives.[23] It is likely that this was true in many of the combined platoons, and considering the extent of the combat experience of many of the PFs, the wise Marines probably learned more from the PFs than they tried to teach them.

Working in the Villages

On August 1, 1965, the Joint Action Company was formally established, and within a few days the platoons began to make daytime patrols through their assigned villages. The Marines had little interaction with the people during this time because the primary purpose of the patrols was to have the Marines become familiar with the areas where they would be working. These daytime patrols were also fairly safe, and they gave the Marines and the PFs a chance to practice their patrolling techniques as a joint unit in safe situations. After the first week, the combined platoons began to stay in the villages at night, and to conduct over twenty night patrols and ambushes each week. The night operations were calculated to make the Marines as familiar with the area as the enemy was. These patrols were also an important step the combined platoons made in keeping the NLF away.

Before the combined platoons were established in the villages the NLF could operate confidently in the area at night because there were few if any PF patrols. At night the NLF often entered the villages to give propaganda lectures, take food, collect taxes, and take recruits for its army. After the combined platoons started to saturate the area with patrols and ambushes at night, the guerrillas had to be more cautious because the Marines and the PFs were now waiting for them.

As the combined platoons took their first steps to protect the Vietnamese people from the NLF, they also started to learn about the NLF operations and how the NLF controlled the people. Ek said he eventually learned the NLF organization in the area was made up of approximately thirty confirmed NLF members with an experienced leader, but there were also NLF sympathizers in the villages. There may have been some women fighters with the local NLF, but Ek said most of the women associated with the enemy were sympathizers. The NLF wanted to control the villages so their forces could collect rice from this rich farming area to send to NLF forces farther to the north. The NLF controlled the people primarily with terror, Ek thought, and if the combined platoons could not protect the people from the NLF, the people would give their allegiance to the guerrillas. NLF retribution could be especially brutal, Ek said, and on occasions the NLF fighters disemboweled people and cut the bodies of others into pieces to make an example of those who cooperated with South Vietnamese government authorities.

What the Marines learned about the NLF organization in the area and its methods to control the population reinforced what they already knew about the NLF. If the combined platoons were going to gain the loyalty of the people and protect them and their rice from the NLF, they needed to both root out the NLF members and sympathizers and keep the NLF from getting into the villages.[24]

Soon after the combined platoons started living in the villages, they began intelligence and population control measures to find and eliminate NLF activities. The Marines were told to talk with the civilians and to watch them as they went about their daily routines. If the behavior of any of the people seemed unusual, or if the daily routines were altered, the Marines were told to find out the reason. Each of the Marines kept a small notebook in which they noted these behaviors and routines, and any changes in them. The notebooks were given to the Marine squad leader on a regular basis, and he compiled the findings in a report he sent on to his commander. Eventually these reports were studied at the headquarters of 3/4 for intelligence purposes. This gave the combined platoons some intelligence information, but the PFs were also able to get good information about the NLF. The people of the villages usually felt more comfortable talking with the PFs, and many of them were relatives or friends.

The National Police in the region were also a good source of information about the NLF, Ek said, and they helped in the identification checks the combined platoons conducted for population control in the villages. For these identification checks a part of a village was blocked off early in the morning, and the people were called out of their homes. The Marines and the PFs would apologize to the people for the inconvenience, but the people were told it was necessary to do this to protect them from the NLF. The National Police then spoke with the people and made sure they all had their government identification cards. The National Police were used for this because they had a better understanding of how to detect NLF agents.

Along with security, intelligence, and population control, psychological operations and civic action were important parts of Ek's plans for the combined action platoons in the villages. The PFs did much of the work for the psychological operations. To do this, the PFs told the people about the successes of the combined platoons in the area, and the information was more believable for the people when it came from the PFs. They told the people the NLF fighters could no longer come to the villages as freely as they had, and the protection of the combined platoons prevented the NLF from taking tax money, rice, and young men for their army. Also, the PFs told the people about any fights the combined platoons had recently won against the NLF forces. The civic action projects the combined platoons initiated were intended to help the economy of the villages and the people generally. Ek said it was important to work on civic action projects the people themselves wanted, and not projects the Marines thought they should want. Among the early civic action projects were building bridges and getting a source of clean water.[25]

After being in existence for a few months, the combined platoons started to show progress in reaching the goals Ek had set for them as a unit. There were no major disagreements between the Marines and the Popular Forces as they lived and worked together. Also, the Marines and the PFs seemed to have created a synthesis of the knowledge of the two groups as they gradually adopted the best of the PF methods and the best of the Marine methods. The constant presence of the combined platoons in the villages improved security, and the large number of day and night patrols they conducted kept NLF fighters away from these areas. A document found on the body of a dead NLF fighter said, "There were at least 4,000 Marines in the area. You could not move anywhere because Marines were always in the way."[26] Most of the Marines in the area were those in the combined platoons, and there were approximately forty of them. However, the reaction of the NLF expressed in this document showed that the aggressive patrolling was inhibiting NLF activity and improving security in the area.

As security improved, more intelligence information about NLF activities was given to the combined platoons by the people. Partly because of this, and partly because of good population control actions, the combined platoons were able to keep many NLF agents out of the villages. In one instance NLF fighters tried to capture a village official at his home, but Marines and PFs knew about the attempt in advance, and they prevented it. Ek said as security kept the NLF away from the villages and as civic action projects brought fresh water, bridges, and other improvements to the lives of the people, the psychological operation efforts to convince the people of the benefits of supporting the combined platoons also became easier.[27]

In October 1965 the name of the Joint Action Company was officially changed to Combined Action Company (CAC). The name was changed because it was determined troops of the same country worked together in "joint" actions, but troops of different countries worked together in "combined" actions. The concern over the name and the changing of the name showed how sensitive the South Vietnamese were to maintaining their independence and to not giving the appearance they were under the control of the United States. The company became the Combined Action Company, and the platoons became Combined Action Platoons (CAPs).[28]

To get a truer picture of how well the CAPs were performing in the first few months of their existence, it is valuable to find out not only what a Marine officer was thinking, but also what a Marine enlisted man was thinking. Hop Brown was an African-American from Harlem who was serving in 3/4 as a Marine rifleman when he was assigned as a member of one of the first combined platoons at Phu Bai. Brown thought the training the Marines received before they lived with the Vietnamese was good because the Marines learned Vietnamese customs, language, and rituals, which helped them understand and respect the people. Initially Brown was shocked by the poor living standards of the villagers, but as he lived among the people and came to know them, he said he sympathized with them and respected their culture. His experience with the PFs was similar; at first, he thought they were in the Popular Forces to avoid service in the ARVN where they would probably be in heavy combat. Eventually Brown came to think they joined the Popular Forces to protect their families from the NLF.[29]

The support his CAP received from the Marine Corps, the ARVN, and from the South Vietnamese government officials was very good, in Brown's opinion. He said the Marine units in the area responded quickly with reaction forces when the CAP asked for help during an NLF attack. Also, he said the Marine Corps gave the unit all the help and support it needed to do its work in the villages. Importantly, the Marine Corps let the platoon use its own judgement to act on any intelligence the platoon had, and the platoon was also allowed to do what it thought was necessary to improve security and win the confidence of the people in the village. Brown also said the platoon received good intelligence information and artillery support from the ARVN, and the National Police helped them with any problems they had in the village.

As time passed, Brown said the Vietnamese villagers began to like and trust the Marines in the CAP. He thought this because the people made the Marines feel welcome in the village, and they started to give the Marines intelligence information about NFL activities around the village. It is interesting that Brown said his best experience in the platoon was making friends with a young Vietnamese boy in the village. He grew close to the boy, and when Brown left the platoon to go home the boy and his family all came to say goodbye to him. This is touching, and it shows the strong friendships that could develop between the Marines and the Vietnamese.

Brown was critical of the platoon in some ways, though. He said he did not volunteer for the duty, and neither did any of the other men who went to the combined platoon in which he served. He was not sure why the others were chosen, but in his case, he thought he was chosen because he was perceived as a discipline problem. Brown may have been an exception, but this contradicts the idea that only the best volunteers were chosen for duty in the combined platoons. Also, Brown did not get along well with his CAP squad leader, who he said was a racist. These could be important problems for someone serving in one of the combined platoons, because of the close proximity in which the men lived and worked.

It is significant that even though Brown did not volunteer for the platoon and he disliked his squad leader, he still valued the experience of serving in the combined platoon. In his opinion there was a strong bond in the platoon that made it almost like a family and he said he did not feel that close to the men with whom he served in other units. Also, he thought the combined platoons were a success because they showed the Vietnamese people the Marines would live in the villages to protect the people and share their dangers. Altogether, it seems as if Brown's service in the combined platoon gave him compassion for the Vietnamese people, and he was proud he protected them.[30]

From the perspective of Ek as the commander of the Combined Action Company, and the perspective of Brown as an enlisted man, the company was making progress in its counter-insurgency job of separating the people from the NLF. However, at a higher level there was a conflict that would affect the CAP program more in the future. Some influential officers in the US Army and the US Marine Corps continued to differ over what they thought were the appropriate strategy and tactics for the war. General Westmoreland of the US Army wanted the Marines to follow his strategy of attrition and the tactics of search and destroy. For their part, Generals Krulak and Walt were US Marine Corps generals who strongly supported an enclave strategy and counterinsurgency methods such as the CAP platoons as best suited for the war. This conflict of approaches was becoming more pronounced.

Two military actions in South Vietnam in November 1965 brought the tactics of the US Army approach and the US Marine Corps approach into sharp contrast. In the southern area of South Vietnam during one day of a search and destroy operation involving almost 25,000 men from five brigades, twenty NLF fighters were killed. Further to the north, in the Phu Bai area, elements of a CAP platoon ambushed an NLF platoon close to the village where the CAP platoon lived. In the ambush, four NLF fighters were killed, and one was captured.[31] The massive effort of the search and destroy operation succeeded in killing only a few of the guerrillas and adding to the total body count for the strategy of attrition. For its part, the CAP ambush helped to keep the NLF separated from the village, and the guerrilla forces were kept away from the food, the intelligence, and the young men for their army they needed from the village if they were to survive.

By the end of November 1965, the CAP program had been in existence for approximately four months, and it looked as if it could develop into a successful counterinsurgency concept in the Vietnam War. The most important reason for this was that the CAPs kept the NLF out of the villages. One reason the security in the villages was strong was that the Marines and the PFs combined their respective strengths to together create a strong platoon capable of finding and defeating NLF forces. As the Marines lived and worked with the PFs in the villages, they gained the trust and the friendship of some of the people because the Marines showed their commitment to help and defend the villages. Also, unlike the NLF, the Marines took nothing from the people. When the people began to trust the Marines, they began to give the Marines intelligence information about NLF activities in the area, and civic action projects brought improvements such as fresh water, schools, and improved medical care to the people. Many of the Vietnamese villagers seemed to be starting to believe they could be safe, and they could live better lives if they supported the CAPs against the NLF, and their support was the most important factor in winning the counterinsurgency war.

Even though the CAPs were showing promise as a counterinsurgency concept, there were early warning signs of problems that would harm them later. The controversy between the US Army and the Marine Corps over strategy and tactics for the war threatened to negatively affect the CAPs if the US Army would not agree to support them. The CAP concept also depended on support from the GVN and the ARVN, and these organizations were increasingly seen as corrupt and unreliable.

Chapter 3

The Early CAPs, Problems, and a Continuing Fight Over Strategy

From the time US troops started fighting in South Vietnam in 1965, the Marine Corps looked for ways to take control of the Vietnamese villages from the NLF guerrillas, and the CAP program showed promise as an important part of the answer. A number of generals in the Marine Corps thought the goal in this counterinsurgency war was obtaining the loyalty of the people, and after operating for a short period of time, the CAP program appeared to be developing as a counterinsurgency concept that could achieve this goal.

By the end of 1965 the CAP program had only been in existence for approximately five months, but it showed the potential to accomplish a number of the goals of counterinsurgency warfare this study sees as necessary for the CAPs to be considered a success. The goal of keeping the guerrillas out of the villages was being pursued with some positive results. The numerous patrols and ambushes the CAPs conducted made them appear to be everywhere and nowhere, throwing the guerrillas off balance in their attempts to enter the villages. There was less food and tax money taken from the people by the guerrillas, and there was less oral and written guerrilla propaganda in the villages. Also, fewer villagers were being forced to join the guerrillas. The goal of gaining the loyalty of the people was being accomplished, to some extent, and an indication of this was that some of the villagers were giving the CAP members intelligence about the guerrillas. Because of this, the CAPs had a better idea of the activities and the size of the local guerrilla units, and they knew who some of the local guerrillas were, although they were not able to find many of them. Still, the presence of the CAPs interfered with the effectiveness of the guerrilla infrastructure. In the area of civic action and economic improvement there were some activities, but most of the CAPs were too busy with their security activities to do much in these areas. Psychological operations were conducted to discredit the guerrillas, and these helped to gain the loyalty and the goodwill of some of the villagers for the CAPs. There were still problems though.

As the CAPs continued to work in the villages, they needed to improve in some important areas of counterinsurgency if they were to succeed. As Robert Thompson told General Krulak, the primary need in a counterinsurgency situation was security for the people of the village. If the people of a village expressed loyalty to the CAPs, and even if they were subject to only a few acts of guerrilla retribution over a period of time, they would not side with the CAPs. If only one person were killed by the guerrillas in retaliation for siding with the CAPs, the people would question whether or not the CAPs could protect them. As a result of this, the security of the villages had to be as complete as possible.

Another priority for the CAPs needed to be the destruction of the guerrilla infrastructure in the villages, because these hidden members of the guerrilla organization ensured the survival of the guerrilla fighters. Also, the members of the guerrilla infrastructure could target villagers who cooperated with the CAPs for intimidation or assassination, and they could perform acts of propaganda and sabotage.[1]

Other areas of counterinsurgency the CAPs needed to stress were civic action and economic development in the villages. The Vietnamese people had to see their lives were materially better under the control of the CAPs than they would be under the control of the guerrillas. A central point of the appeal of a guerrilla movement is usually the promise of a better future under its rule, and if current physical circumstances are good and show promise of becoming even better, then the attraction of the guerrillas' propaganda is lessened considerably.

A factor that helped the CAP program was a belief on the part of many of the Marines who served in the first CAP units that their service in the CAPs was making a worthwhile difference in Vietnam. A Marine who served in one of the first CAPs thought the program was beneficial because the Marines lived in the villages and showed the people the Marines would face the same dangers the villagers faced. This, he said, gained the trust of the Vietnamese villagers, and he considered this part of the reason he thought the CAPs were a success. On a larger scale, the Marines who served in the first CAP units showed their commitment to the objectives of the CAP program when many of them chose to stay with their CAPs rather than leave Vietnam. In December 1965 forty of the sixty-six Marines assigned to the CAPs in the Phu Bai area volunteered to extend their service in Vietnam after their initial tour of duty ended.[2]

Morale in the regular infantry units was strong, but some Marines were becoming frustrated with the way in which the war was being fought. As a Marine infantry officer in 1965, Phillip Caputo said, "By autumn, what had begun as an adventurous expedition had turned into an exhausting, indecisive war of attrition in which we fought for no cause other than our own survival."[3] In contrast, a large number of the Marines in the CAPs at this time appeared to have high morale and a strong sense of purpose because they believed the CAPs were helping the Vietnamese people in particular and the war effort in general.

Many of the CAPs were doing well in the area of counterinsurgency at this point in the war, and it should be emphasized that the PFs in the CAPs were an important reason for this. Some Americans in Vietnam said the PFs fought poorly, but the Marines helped the PFs in this respect. In addition to improving the military training of the PFs, the presence of the Marines also helped their morale. One PF veteran said, "The Americans were so brave that we became brave, too."[4] For their part, the PFs made it possible for the Marines to work in the villages. If the PFs were not in the CAPs, it is doubtful the Marines would have been seen as anything other than an occupying force. Also, many of the PFs had lived in the villages for their entire lives, and some of them had been fighting a guerrilla war throughout the area for years. They taught the Marines the tactics of the guerrillas, and they showed them the trails and the likely ambush sites. Often the PFs served as point men on the CAP patrols because of their knowledge of the area and the enemy. Few of the Marines knew Vietnamese, and because of this they depended on the PFs for much of their communication with the people of the villages. In many instances, the people gave intelligence information to the PFs, who would then pass the information to the Marines. The connection between the PFs and the villagers was close, and one CAP Marine said the PFs in his platoon were related to one hundred and sixty of the two hundred families in the village where the CAP operated.[5] The PFs were truly of the people, and their close connection with the people of the villages, their knowledge of the area, and their knowledge of the guerrillas made the PFs invaluable for the counterinsurgency war.

Vietnam and the Caribbean Wars

This was not the first time Marines served in counterinsurgency units that combined Marines with indigenous troops; it was also done in the counterinsurgency wars the Marine Corps fought in the Caribbean between 1912 and 1933. Officially, Marines were sent to various Caribbean countries during this period to put down insurrections threatening friendly governments and private American and European investments. In the counterinsurgency actions the Marine Corps fought in Haiti, Nicaragua, and Santo Domingo, units made up of Marines and local fighters fought well against guerrilla forces, and this was particularly the case in Santo Domingo where units similar to the CAPs were formed.

In these units a few enlisted Marines and a Marine officer joined with approximately fifteen people from a village to form a village defense force. In addition to helping defend the villages, the Marines trained, organized, and equipped the indigenous fighters. A distinction between these units and the CAPs in Vietnam was that there was not a joint command of the units. Instead, in the mixed units the Marines formed in Haiti, Nicaragua, and Santo Domingo, the Marines were in command. The village defense forces in Santo Domingo did well at keeping the guerrillas out of the villages, and the value of these forces was an important counterinsurgency lesson the Marine Corps learned.[6] Generally, another counterinsurgency lesson the Marine Corps learned in the wars in the Caribbean was that one way Marines could best be utilized was by having them provide leadership and training for the local forces.[7]

The Marine Corps learned a great deal about counterinsurgency warfare in the Caribbean wars, and it started to teach Marines these lessons in a formal setting. In 1920 at the Marine Corps Schools in Quantico, Virginia, the Marine Corps began conducting a series of lectures based on this information.

These practical lectures based on experience were continued over a period of time, and eventually much of the information from the lectures was published as the book, *Small Wars Manual*, in 1940.

Until shortly before the publication of this manual, the Marine Corps saw fighting counterinsurgency wars as its primary mission, and with the exception of US involvement in World War I, fighting counterinsurgency wars in the Caribbean was the mission of the Marine Corps for more than three decades. In fact, during World War I Marines were also involved in counterinsurgency fighting in both Haiti and in Santo Domingo.[8]

Even before the manual was published, though, the primary mission of the Marine Corps was changing. The possibility of war with Japan became a probability, and the Marine Corps was needed as an amphibious assault force to capture island bases for the US in the Pacific Ocean. During World War II the mission of the Marine Corps was to conduct amphibious assaults, and, for the most part, this continued to be the primary mission for the Marine Corps after World War II. Partly because of this, the counterinsurgency techniques distilled in *Small Wars Manual* were largely neglected for a period of time. However, when the Vietnam War began, a number of the highest-ranking generals in the Marine Corps had been young officers before World War II, and some of them remembered the counterinsurgency lessons of the Caribbean wars and looked for ways to apply them in Vietnam.

Victor Krulak was one of these Marine Corps generals who contributed to the development of the strategy and the tactics used by the Marine Corps in the initial stages of the Vietnam War, and it looks as if he used counterinsurgency lessons from the *Small Wars Manual* and the Caribbean. The US needed to use a counterinsurgency strategy in Vietnam, in Krulak's opinion, and in the first few months of the Vietnam War he proposed an enclave strategy to gradually take control of the coastal region on the northeastern coast of South Vietnam. Within the enclaves, Krulak wanted to use CAP units living in the villages to defend the villages from NLF guerrillas who might filter into the enclaves.

It is striking to see how similar Krulak's plan is to a plan of action detailed in the *Small Wars Manual*. In the manual it says a commander may need to secure "A certain area, the economic resources of which are such that its possessor controls the life-blood of the country." This is in keeping with Krulak's idea of controlling the northeastern coastal region of South Vietnam to deprive the NLF guerrillas of the vast amounts of rice grown in that area. The parallels between Krulak's plan and a possible course of action suggested in the manual become even closer, though. The commander is advised that "The entire scheme of maneuver will frequently result in the occupation of the coastal area initially with a gradual coordinated movement inland, thus increasing the territory over which control and protection may be established."[9] Together, these passages from the *Small Wars Manual* can be seen as a summary of Krulak's strategy to create an enclave along the northeastern coast of South Vietnam to keep the NLF away from this heavily populated, rice growing area.

As far as concepts were concerned, it looks as if Krulak found one of his principal concepts for his plan among those used in the Caribbean wars. The manual says that within the enclave, "The area commander … will seek to control his area by use of small detachments to protect the towns and to conduct active operations against irregular groups until the area becomes completely pacified." These detachments could have been made up entirely of Marines, but the manual also says it is beneficial to combine Marines with indigenous troops to improve the leadership and the training of the indigenous forces.[10] In a similar manner, Marines in Vietnam were combined with the PFs to create the CAPs, and the CAPs were used to protect the villages, to train the PFs, and to fight the guerrillas. In considering Krulak's plan, it looks as if he adopted some of the proven counterinsurgency techniques the Marine Corps had developed in the Caribbean wars.

Another of these generals who seems to have used lessons from the Caribbean wars was Lewis Walt, who was given command of the III Marine Amphibious Force in Vietnam in June of 1965. Walt began his career in 1936 when he started his initial training to become an officer in the Marine Corps, and Lewis B. Puller was the captain who commanded Walt's Basic School Company. Puller was a Marine officer who distinguished himself in the fighting in both Haiti and in Nicaragua, especially in Nicaragua. The value of Puller's instructions and example for Walt can be appreciated in looking at Puller's achievements during the remainder of his career in the Marine Corps. Puller went on to become a lieutenant general, and he acquired legendary status as one of the finest Marines to ever wear the uniform. During Walt's training he said Puller often used examples from his experiences in the Caribbean wars in the lectures he gave the officer candidates, and it is probable that some of those lectures were later used in the *Small Manual Wars*. Later in his career Walt expressed great respect for Puller and the lessons he taught him during this initial phase of his training as an officer.[11]

When Walt commanded the III Amphibious Force in Vietnam his actions indicate how great an influence Puller's teaching and the counterinsurgency experiences of the Marine Corps in the Caribbean had on his thinking. Walt thought a counterinsurgency approach to the war would work best, and he saw the allegiance of the Vietnamese people as one of the keys to winning the war. He was a supporter of Krulak's idea of using an enclave strategy, and Walt was the commander who put the enclave strategy into practice. When the idea of forming the first Joint Action Company was being considered, Walt gave it his authorization, and later after the CAP program was having some success, he promoted its expansion. His thinking and his actions show Walt drew on the practical experience of the Marine Corps in the Caribbean to find strategic and operational answers for the war in Vietnam.

Commandant of the Marine Corps Wallace Greene also looked at the Marine Corps experiences in the Caribbean for lessons that could be applied to the war in Vietnam. He had received his commission before World War II, and he was certainly familiar with the information in *Small Wars Manual*. Greene saw the war as a counterinsurgency challenge for the US, and he supported both Krulak's proposal for the use of an enclave strategy and the use of CAP units in Vietnam. Earlier, in 1963, Greene was considering ways the Marine Corps could use its experience in the Caribbean to its benefit in Vietnam. At that time Greene was the Chief of Staff at Headquarters, Marine Corps, and he met with a retired Marine Corps general who had served in the Caribbean wars to ask his advice regarding the question. The retired officer was Edward H. Forney, who had served in Haiti for two years in the 1930s. The advice Forney gave Greene was more pertinent because in 1963 Forney was the Public Safety Advisor with the US Operations Mission in South Vietnam.

In response to Greene's request for advice Forney said he thought the Marine Corps could use its experience in the Caribbean to make a significant contribution in South Vietnam. Forney said the effort "should be a real grass roots level operation … linked with the Civil Guard, the Self Defense Corps, and the local Militia in the village and the boondock level … similar to the Guardia effort in Nicaragua or the Gendarmerie operation in Haiti and Santo Domingo." Forney said he thought these units in the South Vietnamese villages were being neglected at the time, and he thought the people in the villages would welcome a program such as this.[12] Greene's knowledge of Marine Corps counterinsurgency operations in the Caribbean and the advice he received from Forney look as if they were a direct influence on Greene's strong support for the enclave strategy, and for the CAP program.

The Marine Corps was able to draw on a wealth of practical information from the Caribbean wars when it became involved in the Vietnam War, and the influential generals Krulak, Walt, and Greene appear to have used this information to formulate a strategy for the war. Both the enclave strategy and units which combined Marines with indigenous militia forces looked as if they would be appropriate for the situation in Vietnam. It certainly seems wise to use proven methods from the past for current problems.[13] The question was whether or not the CAP idea could be successful in the Vietnam War.

CAP Expansion and Problems

The initial successes of the CAP platoons in the Phu Bai area convinced Marine generals Walt and Krulak that the program should be expanded. Five CAP units were operating around Phu Bai, and in November of 1965 Major General Nguyen Chanh Thi, the ARVN I Corps Commander, agreed to allow eight PF platoons to be placed under Marine control in the Danang region. When he agreed to this transfer, Thi stated that the spirit and the fighting abilities of the PFs were improved by the presence of the Marines in the CAPs. Lieutenant Colonel William W. Taylor, who commanded the Third Battalion of the Fourth Marine Regiment at Phu Bai when the first CAPs were formed, was now the commander of the Third Battalion of the Ninth Marine Regiment at Danang. He used Marines and the PF platoons to form a new Combined Action Company (CAC) to operate in the Danang area.[14]

According to one study, though, few if any of the Vietnamese in one of the first villages where a CAP was located were favorably impressed with the CAPs. James Trullinger wrote *Village at War*, which is a study of the village of My Thuy Phuong in the Phu Bai area, where a CAP unit was stationed. This book was written after the war, and the people may have been reluctant to express their true feelings because they were living under a communist government. Also, during the war Trullinger sympathized with the communist cause. In his book Trullinger said the majority of the people in the village were either actively working with the NLF, or they were sympathetic to the NLF cause . Few of the people remembered much about the CAP except for the fear of being killed by one of the CAP patrols or ambushes. None of the people Trullinger interviewed spoke of any positive relations with CAP members, and none mentioned any civic action projects they had initiated. Rather than seeing the CAP as a military force that protected them from the NLF, the people saw them as another form of US power which opposed the NLF forces the people supported. Trullinger wrote of the people of the village as enduring and opposing the CAP as another manifestation of the war against the NLF, and the villagers said the CAP was not successful in turning the people against the NLF.

Some of the information in Trullinger's book implies the CAP may have been more successful in its counterinsurgency war in the My Thuy Phuong region than Trullinger acknowledges, though. He quotes from a captured NLF document in which an NLF commander said the psychological warfare information directed at the NLF "created dissention among our forces and various religious sects … [and] aroused nostalgia among our soldiers and cadres…." This suggests the CAP psychological warfare was working well to divide support for the NLF, and to capitalize on CAP successes to weaken the morale of NLF guerrillas. The NLF commander went on to explain, "the reason why shortcomings rose to a high degree was because of the enemy's stepped-up activities in various fields and … Because of the above shortcomings our cadres were incapable of controlling the people and restoring security in the liberated area ..." This can be seen as meaning the CAP units were doing well in their fights with the NLF guerrillas. Also, it could mean the CAPs were keeping the guerrillas out of the villages, and the villagers were turning to the CAPs for protection. Another quoted NLF document stated the guerrillas "have not satisfactorily performed fighting, protection of the villages, people and agricultural production. They have not carried out the role of being a backbone of the people's political struggle and of the resupply of concentrated units."[15]

This could mean the CAPs were keeping the guerrillas out of the villages and away from the people. It could also mean the CAPs were gaining the loyalty of some of the people, and the villagers were not willing to supply the guerrillas with food and recruits the guerrillas needed. The information in these documents is not conclusive, but it shows the NLF was having setbacks during this time, and a contributing factor for this was probably the presence and the counterinsurgency activities of the CAPs. Despite initial signs of success, the CAP program faced formidable problems, however.

One such problem was the growing conflict between the US Army and the Marine Corps over the most appropriate strategy and tactics for the war. William Westmoreland had previously given the Marines commanded by Walt in I Corps some freedom of interpretation for his orders, but he was becoming more impatient with the Marines by November of 1965. Westmoreland was concerned that in I Corps the Marine strategy left the "enemy free to come and go as he pleased throughout the bulk of the region."

To add to Westmoreland's concern, US Army Brigadier General William DePuy, the MACV operations officer, went to I Corps in November and was displeased with the situation he found there. DePuy reported to Westmoreland that he was "disturbed by the fact that all but a tiny part of the I Corps area is under the control of the VC [Viet Cong] who have freedom of movement east and west—north and south—outside the Marine enclaves." He also thought the NLF guerrillas in the area were growing stronger and the ARVN troops were not able to contain this threat. DePuy went on to say "the Vietnamese cannot adequately fill in behind the Marines in their expanding enclaves and for this reason, the Marines are stalled a short distance south of Danang." As a result of this, DePuy said, "If they move out farther, they will have insecure areas behind them for which there are no Regional or Popular forces or pacification cadre to provide long term hamlet-by-hamlet security."[16] This report reinforced Westmoreland's opinion that the Marines should be more aggressive, and he pushed them to conduct more search and destroy operations beyond the established enclaves.

Some of Westmoreland's concerns had merit, but others were a matter of different strategic approaches to the war. The Marines did not want to engage in random search and destroy operations beyond the limits of the enclaves. Instead, they sent numerous small patrols into the areas outside the enclave in an effort to find the main force units of the NLF and the NVA. When good intelligence was developed as to the location of the main force NLF units, the Marines could then strike an identified target with sufficient force to give the Marines the advantage in the fight. The Marines thought this method was better than having their battalions randomly move through the jungle in a search for hidden NLF and NVA units.

DePuy's conclusions regarding the inability of the ARVN, the RFs, and the PFs to provide security in the enclaves was in keeping with the conclusions the Marines drew themselves. By this time the Marines had attempted a number of ways to use the ARVN, the RFs, and the PFs in hamlet security within the enclaves, but none of them worked well. One promising way the Marines were providing security was the CAP program, which combined Marines with PFs, and it is unfortunate DePuy's inspection of the Danang area was conducted in the same month the CAP program was authorized to expand to the region around Danang. If DePuy saw the CAPs after they had been operating in the villages around Danang for a period of time, he probably would have been more favorably impressed with the security within the enclaves.

Westmoreland did not like the idea of using the CAP concept widely, and this was partly because he saw an ARVN program similar to the CAPs fail badly. In Binh Dinh province in 1964 Westmoreland suggested that small units of ARVN troops be assigned to the districts in the province for security and for patrolling throughout the area. After the plan was put into practice, it worked well for a period of time. Eventually, though, two NLF regiments conducted an offensive in the area and defeated each of the small ARVN forces. Part of the reason the NLF units were able to do this was that the ARVN did not have battalion and regimental units of their own in reserve for reinforcements. The conclusion Westmoreland drew from these events was that the large NLF units had to be destroyed before small ARVN or US units could be safely used for security and pacification duties. Otherwise, in Westmoreland's thinking, the small units would be too vulnerable to defeat by the NLF main force battalions and regiments.[17]

The Marine Corps did not agree with Westmoreland's idea that the CAP concept should be abandoned because of the vulnerability of the small CAP units; instead the Marines resolved to correct the weakness. The Marines thought the counterinsurgency work the CAPs were doing was critical for keeping the guerrillas out of the villages, and rather than eliminating the program because of its exposure to attacks by large NLF units, they resolved the problem by having infantry forces ready to reinforce the CAPs. In many situations this worked well. In one instance when a large force of NLF guerrillas attacked one of the first CAPs, a Marine said an infantry unit quickly came to reinforce the CAP in the fight.

In his book, *A Soldier Reports*, Westmoreland gave faint praise for the CAPs, but he also showed he did not fully understand how the CAP concept was used by the Marines. The CAP program was an innovative pacification program, Westmoreland said, and he sent information about their successes to units under his command. Those units were told they could use their own judgement in using the CAP idea where they thought it would be appropriate. As far as using CAPs more widely in South Vietnam was concerned, though, Westmoreland was against the idea. He said, "I simply had not enough numbers to put a squad of Americans in every village and hamlet; that would have been fragmenting resources and exposing them to defeat in detail."[18] However, the Marine Corps intended to solve the weakness of CAPs as isolated units by having reaction forces close to the CAP villages. Also, the Marines only wanted the CAPs to be located in enclaves in the heavily populated, rice-growing regions of the northeastern coastal area of I Corps and the Mekong Delta. A large number of troops would have been needed to create a network of CAPs in this area, but Westmoreland's comments show he did not understand how the Marine Corps intended to use the CAPs as a counterinsurgency concept.

When the Marine Corps expanded the CAPs in November 1965 the attitude of the US Army toward the program turned from disapproval to active resistance. The Marine Corps was told that no additional assigned quotas of Marines would be provided for the support of the CAP program, and "If you want to play around with such foolishness you'll have to eat the personnel spaces out of your own hide." This was a serious problem for the Marine Corps because it meant any men assigned to the CAPs would have to be taken from Marine infantry units, and those units needed every man they had. Regardless, some infantry commanders were willing to assign their men to the CAPs because they believed the CAPs were serving a worthwhile purpose.[19]

The US Army's decision to not provide additional Marines for the CAP program had a negative effect on the ability of the CAPs to perform their counterinsurgency role. The CAPs were intended to have a squad of fourteen Marines with a Navy Corpsman, and a PF platoon of approximately thirty-five men. In fact, though, there were usually fewer than thirty-five PFs available for the CAPs. This force of approximately forty-nine men was responsible for keeping the guerrillas out of Vietnamese villages with populations which could be larger than five thousand people. As they searched for the NLF guerrillas, the CAP members patrolled through and around the villages which often covered areas of ten square miles or more. In addition to keeping the guerrillas away from the villages, the CAPs were also responsible for other counterinsurgency duties such as accomplishing civic action projects, gathering intelligence, and psychological warfare operations.

Performing these missions with a squad of fourteen men, a corpsman, and a force of PFs would be difficult, but the reality was that the CAPs often had ten or fewer Marines and a corpsman. The lack of support from the US Army meant there were fewer Marines available for the CAPs, and this meant the CAPs could not perform their counterinsurgency missions as well as they could have with more Marines. The Marine infantry units provided some of their men for the CAPs, but the infantry units needed every man they had, and this was especially the case when the Marines began fighting pitched battles with the NVA in the Demilitarized Zone (DMZ) region in 1966.

After the United States had been fighting in Vietnam for over eight months, Krulak submitted a second strategic appraisal of the war in December 1965 in which he expressed his dissatisfaction. Krulak said that while the strategy for the war was never clearly stated, he saw it as one of attrition which intended to "attrit the enemy to a degree which makes him incapable of prosecuting the war, or unwilling to pay the cost of so doing." He went on to say, "If this is indeed the basis for our strategy, it has to be regarded as inadequate." Krulak thought the strategy of attrition attacked the strength in manpower of the NVA and the NLF and neglected their material weaknesses. The North Vietnamese and the NLF had thousands of soldiers to send into the fight in South Vietnam. If the United States fought a war of attrition against these forces it would result in unacceptable levels of casualties for the United States, regardless of the number of NVA and NLF soldiers killed. Krulak pointed out that at the ratio of NVA and NLF casualties to US casualties at this point in the war, ten thousand Americans would be killed in order to kill 20 percent of the NVA and NLF soldiers.

The strength of the NVA and the NLF was in the number of soldiers they could put into the fight, and Krulak made a radical proposal to attack the material weakness of their forces. He saw the NVA and the NLF as vulnerable in a material sense because the military supplies and the fuel they needed to conduct the war came into North Vietnam through its harbors and over its railways from China. In Krulak's opinion, the NVA and NLF war effort in South Vietnam could be severely hurt if the North Vietnamese harbor facilities were bombed, the harbors mined, and the railways from China bombed. Cutting off the supplies the NVA and the NLF needed to fight the war in South Vietnam had the power to cripple their ability to fight, and Krulak saw this as a key element of the strategy he thought was needed to win the war.[20]

Instead of fighting the war with a strategy of attrition, Krulak said the United States should use a strategy based on counterinsurgency, which separated the people of South Vietnam from the NLF guerrillas and gave the people security to protect them from the NLF. In the strategic proposal he wrote in June 1965 Krulak had said pacification operations should be a primary consideration, and in his December assessment he continued to think pacification should be emphasized. He also thought the

US military should be used for pacification, because the South Vietnamese government and the ARVN had shortcomings which could not be overcome very soon.

In I Corps the Marine Corps created Joint Coordinating Councils, which formed one authority over all the South Vietnamese and US civilian and military pacification efforts in their regions. One benefit of these councils was that they made it possible to create one clear plan. Krulak thought councils such as these should be put into place in South Vietnam from Saigon down to the level of the various corps regions.

Krulak restated his belief in the enclave strategy when he said US military forces should pacify areas adjacent to their enclaves to form larger pacified areas in South Vietnam. To make pacification more effective, he said all US units that were in contact with Vietnamese civilians should be given specific standards for civic action programs they were to conduct.[21]

The ideas in Krulak's strategic appraisal show he was frustrated with what he saw as a failing strategy of attrition he thought should be replaced with an enclave strategy emphasizing pacification. He said the loyalty and the support of the Vietnamese people was vital for winning the war, and there was too little being done in the area of pacification to gain the loyalty and the support of these people. Many of the victories in battles against the NVA and the NLF main force units were meaningless, in his opinion, and he thought it was more important to keep the NVA and the NLF away from the Vietnamese villages. Regarding the war of attrition he said, "A key point is this: the conflict between the North Vietnamese/ hard core Vietcong, on the one hand, and the US, on the other, could move to another planet today and we would not have won the war." He then gave a primary reason for focusing on pacification to keep the NVA and the NLF away from the populated areas of South Vietnam, when he said, "On the other hand, if the subversion and guerrilla efforts were to disappear, the war would soon collapse, as the enemy would be denied food, sanctuary and intelligence."

A large number of US troops would be needed for the work among the Vietnamese people in a war based on pacification, in Krulak's opinion, but he thought fewer troops would be needed than were being used for the search and destroy operations in support of the attrition strategy. Also, he thought the number of US casualties would be fewer. Krulak's statements demonstrated his conviction that a spreading enclave strategy with a focus on pacification might bring the war to a successful conclusion for the US, and his belief that a strategy based on attrition could only result in the war's being lost.[22]

In the conclusion of the paper Krulak recommended actions he thought were needed for victory. The focus of the war needed to be on defeating the NLF guerrillas and on providing security to keep the guerrillas away from the Vietnamese people. As this was being done, the main force NLF and NVA units would be attacked when firm intelligence located them, and when the situation was in favor of US forces. Also, the North Vietnamese port facilities, industrial sites, fuel depots, power plants, and rail lines should be destroyed, and the ports mined. In keeping with his emphasis on pacification, Krulak said all appropriate US and Vietnamese resources needed to be used for pacification and the PFs should be given more training by US forces. US military units which had contact with the Vietnamese civilians needed to concentrate on developing civic action programs to be conducted among the people. In his last recommendation Krulak said the Vietnamese government should be pressured to initiate an extensive program of land reform.

The conclusion of the paper ended with two points which illustrated Krulak's belief that a change in strategy was imperative to prevent a catastrophic end to the US war effort. First, he stressed the US needed a military strategy that took into consideration the political, the social, and the economic conditions in South Vietnam. In other words, he was promoting a strategy that emphasized counterinsurgency and pacification, and not attrition. Second, he said the strength of the NLF and the NVA was in the number of soldiers they had, and the strategy of attrition was attacking their strength, and not their weaknesses. He ended by bluntly saying these two factors had to be the basis for a change in strategy, and if the current strategy of attrition were continued, the war would end in a defeat for the United States.

This paper was Krulak's analysis of the strategy of the war, and he did not mention the CAP program specifically. However, he expressed how important he thought it was to protect the people from the NLF guerrillas, and to keep the guerrillas from getting the rice, the intelligence, and the recruits they could get in the villages. Also, he made the point that he thought US forces should be used to train the PFs who defended the villages.[23] The CAP concept was considered successful enough to expand the program at approximately the time Krulak wrote his paper, and these two ideas were among the primary missions of the CAPs. As the CAP program was expanded, the CAPs eventually became an integral part of the pacification plan the Marine Corps used in its enclaves.

Because he was deeply concerned about the way the war was being fought, Krulak made a determined attempt to have his strategic plan adopted. Initially, Krulak took it to Admiral Ulysses S.G. Sharp, Commander-in-Chief, Pacific, who said he liked it, and gave Krulak permission to show the plan to Marine Commandant Greene. After Greene said he thought the plan was good, he told Krulak he should present it to Secretary of Defense Robert S. McNamara. The relationship between Krulak and McNamara was good because they had worked well together during 1962–1964 when Krulak had served on the Joint Staff as the special assistant for counterinsurgency and special activities. After listening to Krulak's plan, McNamara's primary concern seems to have been with the bombing and the mining of the North Vietnamese ports and the bombing of the railways to China. Eventually, Krulak was able to present his plan to President Lyndon Johnson, and Johnson listened as Krulak explained it to him. When Krulak said the US needed to bomb the North Vietnamese port facilities and mine the ports, Johnson rose to his feet and showed Krulak to the door. Johnson and others in the US government thought bombing and mining in North Vietnam on the scale Krulak's plan proposed would risk bringing Russia, China, or both, into the war.[24] Partly because this one aspect of Krulak's plan was seen as too extreme, it looks as if the entire plan was rejected.

The US was clearly not willing to start a war with either the Soviet Union or The People's Republic of China over Vietnam. Whether the Soviet Union and China were willing to go to war with the US over Vietnam is more obscure, though. Both the Soviet Union and China provided North Vietnam with extensive material and technical assistance during the course of the war. For its part, China sent a tremendous amount of military and economic aid to North Vietnam , and China also sent approximately five hundred thousand troops and technical and military advisors to North Vietnam. The threat of China's entering the war was a major reason the US did not invade North Vietnam.[25]

However, the former NVA officer Bui Tin thought neither the Soviet Union nor China were willing to fight the US if North Vietnam were invaded, and he said both countries let the North Vietnamese know this was the case. The North Vietnamese thought the US might invade if they knew this, though, and they continued to say the Soviet Union and China would help them if the US invaded.[26]

Krulak understood the inherent risks in his plan to bomb and mine North Vietnamese ports and to bomb railways to China, but this plan needs to be considered within the context of the situation. The US was engaged in a war, and it was Krulak's duty as a military officer to contribute to victory in the war. He saw the US strategy of attrition as mistaken because it attacked the NLF and NVA strengths, and he thought continuing to pursue this strategy would result in a bloody defeat for the US. Instead, Krulak proposed to attack the NLF and NVA weaknesses by blocking the NLF and the NVA from the food and the recruits they needed. To fight the war, the NLF and the NVA also needed rockets, artillery, antiaircraft guns, and other weaponry and supplies transported to South Vietnam from North Vietnam. These weapons and other supplies for the war first entered North Vietnam through its ports and over the rail lines from China. If this flow of supplies into North Vietnam could be stopped, the ability of the NLF and the NVA to fight would be severely constrained.

Instead of using a strategy of attrition to attack their strength in manpower, Krulak proposed to attack these two weaknesses of the NLF and the NVA. He saw this as a calculated risk, but he said, "I was sure the Russians were not about to start a war with the United States over Indochina and that, if put to the test, the North Vietnamese would probably prefer having Americans in their country to Chinese, whom they hate." There was the element of a desperate gamble in Krulak's plan, but the war was a bloody stalemate at the time he conceived his idea, and the only alternative he could see for his plan's adoption was a painful defeat for the US.[27]

As a consequence of Krulak's strategic plan not being either wholly or partially adopted, the strategy of attrition with its search and destroy operations continued to dominate the Vietnam War. Later studies done during the war proposed changes similar to those in Krulak's strategic proposal. As for the CAP program, the US Army continued to endorse a strategy of attrition, and to deny the Marine Corps support needed to improve the ability of the CAPs to perform their counterinsurgency duties.

Adjusting to the Village Culture

The CAP program expanded, though, and adjusting to the culture in the villages was a challenge the Marines faced. An African-American CAP Marine from Harlem said, "I didn't think I'd ever see people living in more squalid and degrading conditions than what I'd left behind."[28] The poverty and the living standards of the Vietnamese were initially shocking for many Marines. The Marines also found it difficult to accept that the Vietnamese habitually defecated in front of their homes and in other public areas, and at other times the Vietnamese defecated in the rice paddies to fertilize the rice crop. This was disconcerting for the Marines, and the sexual habits in these rural villages could also be upsetting. The Vietnamese strictly prohibited premarital sex between men and women, but masturbation between men was commonly accepted. It was hard for some Marines to have respect and sympathy for the people when cultural habits such as these were so different from those in the United States.

To work and be accepted in the villages, the Marines needed to understand and appreciate how important the elderly were in Vietnamese culture. It was easy for the Marines to play and joke with the children who were open and friendly, but they learned it was more important to be respectful toward the elderly in the village, and to spend time talking with them. The Marine squad leader especially had to cultivate a good relationship with the village chief and the district chief, if possible. To gain the goodwill of these men, the squad leader might have tea with them and ask their opinions on various matters. Gaining the favor of these men gave the CAP status among the villagers.[29] The reverse was true also; if the village chief and the district chief were opposed to the CAPs, then the CAPs had a difficult time accomplishing much.

Learning the nuances of a foreign culture was a delicate process for the Marines, and a small mistake could create large problems. In some instances, the Vietnamese were offended by actions of the Marines that were a result of Marine ignorance of Vietnamese cultural values. When the Marines spoke with the Vietnamese children, they would often pat the children affectionately on the head, but the Marines learned the Vietnamese thought this brought bad luck to the children. Also, according to the beliefs of some Vietnamese, if a person crossed his legs and the heel of his crossed leg pointed at someone, that person would soon die. Mistakes such as these which resulted from cultural ignorance seem trivial, but they could alienate the villagers and frustrate the CAP efforts to gain the loyalty of the people in the villages.

As the Marines attempted to acquire sensitivity to the culture of the villages, they also worked to sharpen the skills necessary to fight the NLF in a counterinsurgency war. To do this, the Marines and the PFs trained to work together as a military unit. The Marines also had other work, such as giving the PFs additional training, finding a way to acquire intelligence, performing civic action, and conducting psychological warfare actions. For these and other reasons, finding a way to make the CAP concept work well was a tremendous challenge, and how well the CAPS were performing their counterinsurgency tasks at this early point in their development is a critical question.

Chapter 4

Evaluation of Early CAP Performance

In this formative period of the CAP program, the Marines and the PFs trained and worked together to sharpen the skills needed to defeat the NLF in a counterinsurgency war. The Marines tried to find better methods to acquire intelligence, perform civic action, and conduct psychological warfare actions. For these and other reasons, finding a way to make the CAP concept work well was a great challenge. How well the CAPs were performing their counterinsurgency tasks at this early point in their development is an important question.

When the CAP program began, the Marines chosen for the program were usually carefully picked volunteers, but these high standards were difficult to maintain as the program expanded. In the first CAP platoons Lieutenant Paul Ek formed in the Phu Bai area in 1965 he was able to personally choose the men he thought were appropriate for the job. He understood the difficult counterinsurgency mission he wanted the CAPs to accomplish, and he looked for men with qualities he thought were important for accomplishing the mission. Ek said he chose "Men who were mature, intelligent, who possessed leadership capabilities and tact."

He emphasized, though, that "tact was the most important qualification." Also, Ek stressed that the men he chose for the CAPs had to be motivated to work with the Vietnamese people, and to respond to the needs of the people.[1]

When the CAP program was expanded, though, the additional men had to be taken from the existing strength of the Marine infantry units because no specific quotas were created for CAP units. The infantry commanders were told to select men for transfer to the CAPs who were "mature and highly motivated," but this caused a conflict of interest for the infantry commanders. In effect, they were asked to send some of their best enlisted men and non-commissioned officers (NCOs) to the CAP program, and this would weaken the combat effectiveness of their own units. This was particularly true because some of the infantry battalions were told to send as many as thirty of their men to the CAP program each month. Because sending their best men to the CAPs would lessen the combat strength of their units, and because the description of men needed for the program was open to interpretation, the infantry commanders sometimes sent the men they did not want in their units to the CAPs.[2]

The quality of the Marines in the program was important for the success of the CAP counterinsurgency mission, and it is revealing to look at how some Marines became assigned during this early period. For various reasons, a number of the Marines sent to the CAPs during the expansion of the program were "volunteered" by their units. One Marine said he was not asked if he wanted to go to CAPs, and he did not volunteer. He said he was seen as a loner in his company, and when he got into a fight with another Marine, he was quickly transferred to the CAPs. Private First Class (PFC) David Sherman was in a platoon ordered to provide men to go to CAPs. After approximately half the needed men volunteered, Sherman and a number of other men were told they would also go to the CAPs. Sherman did not want to go, and he did not volunteer. He went, as he said, with "No school, no indoctrination, no nothing. Gather a bunch of Marines, stick us outside a hamlet, and we were a CAP."

In another instance, PFC Thomas Flynn was a member of a battalion scheduled to rotate from Vietnam in 1966. Flynn and some other Marines who had not been in Vietnam for very long were told they would stay in Vietnam and be assigned to the CAP program. Flynn said he never heard of the program before he was told he would become a part of it.[3] These experiences show some of the more questionable ways men went to the CAP program, but they were probably the exceptions.

Most of the men who went to the CAP program did volunteer and many volunteered because they wanted to help the Vietnamese people, and they thought the CAP program would help win the war. Jim Donovan went to a CAP when his battalion commander requested, "volunteers, and good ones" from the companies under his command. Donovan said he was personally chosen by the battalion commander, and he helped to choose the other men for the CAPs from among those who volunteered. He said, "They were all good, and not a 'bird' in the bunch." After serving in an infantry company Sergeant Mac McGahan volunteered for duty in a CAP unit because he wanted to help the Vietnamese people. In the CAPs "We can see the progress being made," he said. In his CAP "Eight out of the fourteen men here have extended for another six months."

In McGahan's opinion serving in the CAPs had more purpose than serving in an infantry unit because "In a line company you're in a lot of combat and you're always tired. You don't really care about the people. You just want to put in your time and get out." In the CAPs the war was different, though, because, "Here with the CAP you're not just killing the VC, you're helping people and you can see the progress you're making."[4]

Even those Marines who did volunteer for the CAPs were sometimes not well-suited for the intricate counterinsurgency processes in the villages, though. Some of the Marines who volunteered knew little about the CAPs, but they thought living in the villages was preferable to the grinding violence and danger of serving in an infantry unit. While their intentions may have been good, many of these men were simply too scarred from their previous experiences of fighting the NVA and the NLF main units. They served in areas where they saw very few Vietnamese civilians, and most of the Vietnamese they saw were NVA and NLF fighters. It was difficult to shift from seeing all Vietnamese as enemies, and to now see the villagers as people they were trying to help. One Marine said, "We've been up in the mountains where it's been kill, kill, kill; now we come down here and are told we're supposed to love them all. It's too much to ask."[5] There were also some men who volunteered for the CAPs because they saw living in the villages as better than serving in an infantry unit, but they had a racial hatred for the Vietnamese people. When men such as these were placed in CAPs their intentional or unintentional actions could ruin a bond of cooperation and trust developed over a period of months.[6]

The difficulty of obtaining acceptable volunteers created fundamental problems for the CAP program. The primary reason for this was that the CAPs needed good Marines, and good Marines were needed everywhere. As a result of this some of the Marines sent to the CAPs were cast-offs from the infantry, and they were not good candidates for the program. The Marines sent to the CAPs who either could not or would not serve well in the program were transferred out of a CAP, but this often meant the CAP would be short of the men needed to accomplish its mission. These paradoxes meant the selection process for CAP Marines at this time worked as a detriment for the counterinsurgency work the CAPs were doing in the villages.

An independent study of the CAP program commissioned by the Office of Naval Research was conducted in 1969. A conclusion of that study was that the junior enlisted men chosen for the CAPs were important, but much of the success or failure of the CAPs depended on the Marine squad leader. Throughout the existence of the program, "The major variable affecting the performance of military operations is the leadership ability of the Marine squad leader. This man is the key to the entire operation and on his capabilities all else hinges." If the squad leader had the respect of his men the CAP did its work well, but if the squad leader lost the respect of his men the CAP, "goes slack and becomes not only ineffectual or a liability, but also quite vulnerable to the enemy."[7] The principal reason the squad leader was so important in the CAPs was the sheer physical isolation of the CAP units. The morale of the Marines could become low if they focused on the fact that they were alone in a hostile area. On the other hand, discipline might become a problem when there was little guerrilla activity and the men saw little reason for the constant boredom of patrolling and setting ambushes. In situations such as these the squad leader had to stay motivated and disciplined, and he had to keep his men motivated and disciplined, also.[8] Because the squad leaders were such a vital part of the CAPs, it is revealing to look more closely at who they were.

There were one hundred-eleven CAP platoons at the time of the study in 1969, and over 50 percent of the CAP squad leaders were twenty-one years old or younger, and three of those under twenty-one were eighteen years old. Over 60 percent of them were sergeants, and the others were either corporals or lance corporals. Even though the lance corporals were below NCO rank they were given command of the squads. More than 25 percent of these squad leaders had served in the Marine Corps for less than two years, and the average length of service in the Marine Corps for all of them was less than four years. Approximately half of the men were promoted to their squad leader positions from within the CAP program, and over 40 percent of the squad leaders extended their tour of duty at least one time.[9] One of the most striking impressions taken from this information is that some very young men were given great responsibility to accomplish the complicated and dangerous counterinsurgency missions of the CAPs. The dedication of these men is also impressive. Over forty-four of the squad leaders extended their tour of duty to serve with the CAP program.

The importance of the squad leaders was further confirmed when the study determined an excellent squad leader could improve a mediocre squad to the point that the squad could do a good job. In some instances, the best squad leaders were sent to CAP units where there were problems. As a result of these findings, every effort needed to be made to find the best possible NCOs for the CAP program.[10]

The CAP program was not provided with a steady supply of qualified and highly motivated volunteers and the program would have been more successful if it was given those volunteers. The important job of establishing a bond with the Vietnamese could be ruined by the actions of one man who was less than willing to work closely with the people. However, those Marines who did not, or could not, perform well were quickly transferred out of the program. The central problem, though, was that the same qualified and highly motivated men needed in the CAPs were also needed in the infantry, and the infantry was the primary source of Marines for the CAPs. This was especially true for the quality NCOs needed to command the CAP units, because good NCOs were always at a premium, and few infantry units were willing to release these men if they had a choice. MACV's refusal to give the Marine Corps additional manpower quotas for the CAP units was part of the reason for a lack of qualified Marines for the CAP program. The end result was that the CAP program had too few qualified men, and the CAPs usually had too few men, altogether.

Evaluation of Early CAP Performance of Counterinsurgency Tasks

As the CAP program expanded in 1966, a general pattern was established for the counterinsurgency operations of the CAPs in the villages. The primary responsibility of the CAPs was to provide security to keep the guerrillas out of the villages, and most of the time and the energy of the CAPs was taken up with planning, conducting, and reporting on the ambushes and patrols the CAP performed to provide that security. With good security all the other counterinsurgency goals can be accomplished, but without good security no counterinsurgency goals can be achieved. The patrol is the "lifeblood of security" for all infantry, and this was particularly true for the CAPs. As an infantryman patrols, he "gathers intelligence, projects power, assesses terrain, calms friends, intimidates enemies, outwits the enemy soldier or insurgent who would like to kill him, and, if necessary, gets into a life-and-death fight with that enemy combatant."[11] This definition is a good summary of the purposes of the patrols for the CAPs, and the patrols and the ambushes were the base of the security function for the CAPs in the villages. Frequently the patrols and ambushes were based on intelligence received from the people. The ambushes were small groups of PFs and Marines who hid in the night at points where they thought the guerrillas might pass by them. By conducting a constant series of patrols and ambushes the CAPs worked to take the initiative away from the guerrillas whose strength was that they might attack at any time, and at any place.

If the CAPs began to execute fewer patrols and ambushes during a period of guerrilla inactivity, they could later pay in blood for their lack of attention. Because of this, there was a requirement for each CAP to conduct at least one patrol or ambush each day, and at least two each night. Each of these activities needed to be planned at least three days in advance because they were coordinated with units in the area which provided reaction forces and artillery and mortar fire support. This coordination also prevented the possibility of accidentally firing on friendly units operating in the same area.[12]

The ambushes and the patrols were usually assumed to be planned each day by the Marine squad leader and the platoon sergeant of the PFs. It was thought this joint planning of military activities would help to improve the leadership ability of the PF platoon sergeant. In most of the CAPs this was not done, though. Instead, the Marines planned the activities and then submitted the plans to their headquarters. Shortly before the ambushes and the patrols were sent out in the evening, the PFs were told where they would be going, and what they would be doing. A primary reason for doing this was to prevent anyone's telling the guerrillas the CAP's plans. On some occasions the guerrilla responses to the military activities indicated they knew where the patrols and the ambushes were located, and the most immediate way to deal with the potential problem of a breach in security was to keep the plans a secret until the last minute. Many of the CAPs reported security leaks such as these.

Another reason the Marines planned in this way was to avoid disputes with the PFs. Disputes of this sort took place frequently, and often they seemed to occur because the leader of the PFs wanted to show his authority. When disputes such as these arose, the Marine squad leader either agreed to changes proposed by the PF leader, or he negotiated a compromise plan. In this way the critical idea of the sharing of power between the Marine squad leader and the PF leader was maintained, and there was no loss of face for the PF leader. The reality of having the two leaders in the CAP share power could create problems, but it was important for the morale of the unit, and it was especially important for the morale of the PFs.[13]

The danger of NLF members infiltrating the PF ranks was a constant problem, and the CAP members always needed to be aware of this. After one fight the body of a PF was found among the bodies of the enemy dead.[14] On another occasion a number of PFs led a guerrilla unit through the defenses of a CAP for an attack on the CAP unit. In some villages the PFs helped to keep this problem in check, though. If it became known a PF was disloyal, and if he fled the area, there could be retribution against his family. Measures such as these, and constant vigilance helped to lessen the problem, but the danger of NLF infiltrators among the PFs was never eliminated.

Differences of opinion between the Marines and the PFs over plans for military operations caused problems, but they could be worthwhile, also. If the differences became too great, they could alienate the Marines and the PFs from each other, and their operations could reach a state of near paralysis. If the differences were discussed, and if compromises were achieved, it could work for the benefit of the CAP unit as a whole. The Marines knew good patrolling and ambush techniques, and they practiced them well. However, the PFs were often more experienced in fighting the guerrillas, and they knew the area better than the Marines did. In one instance a PF platoon sergeant took command of the Marines and the PFs in a CAP and led them in defeating a night attack by the guerrillas. The platoon sergeant's bravery and his knowledge of the guerrillas' tactics were instrumental in his ability to do this[15]. The joint command of the CAP was an awkward arrangement, but the unit was more effective when the Marine squad leader and the PF platoon sergeant listened to each and compromised on their plans.

The military activity during the day for the CAPs was almost always a patrol, which served a number of purposes. A primary purpose was to reassure the people with the presence of the CAPs, and to show the villagers the CAPs were vigilant and in control. The patrols in the day were conducted more as general surveillance of the areas, and they were frequently used to train the PFs and Marines who were new to the CAPs. The patrols moved through their area to look for any unusual activity, and to look for any strangers among the people of the villages. Also, the patrols looked for possible locations for future ambushes, and possible routes for future patrols. An important purpose of these patrols was to mingle with the people, and to establish good relations with them. On some occasions a patrol would stop to treat a sick villager, or to help a farmer with his work. As they talked with the people the CAP members were sometimes told of a problem someone had, or they were given intelligence information. The day patrols were only for two hours or less, and after they ended the PFs went to their homes to rest or to work, and most of the Marines returned to their compound to work there and to rest.[16]

At dusk the PFs returned to the CAPs compounds, and the Marines and the PFs began to prepare for the night ambushes and patrols. Men were then assigned to the various missions, the plans were discussed and finalized, and the men cleaned their weapons and prepared their equipment. As night began to fall the patrols left the compound on their missions, and the remainder of the men stayed in defensive positions in the CAP compound. The numbers could vary depending on the mission and the number of men in the platoon, but each patrol was usually comprised of two to four Marines and four to eight PFs. Two patrols were often sent out to set ambushes at previously determined locations where it was thought guerrilla activity might be detected during the night. Later in the night the first patrols usually returned to the compound, and other patrols were sent out to set ambushes. At other times patrols set ambushes and then moved to another ambush position a few hours later. In this way a larger area was covered, and the guerrillas were less sure of where the ambush might be located.[17]

In a guerrilla war the guerrillas usually operate at night when there is less chance of their movement being detected, and they can attack and retreat with less chance of being pursued.

This was the method of the NLF in the Vietnamese villages, and because of this the CAPs needed to be excellent at the skills of night patrols and ambushes.

Learning these skills took courage and determination. His first experience on a night patrol in one of the villages was unnerving for a Marine squad leader who said, "You had the idea the VC were fussing with your mind, that they knew exactly where you were, that they could read the label on a suit in a dark closet." Before he transferred to a CAP the squad leader served in an infantry unit which fought NVA and NLF main force troops, but his experiences on the patrol gave him great respect for the guerrillas: "They're good, man, they're very good. It's their turf."[18] Small, vicious fights in the night were where the war in the villages was fought, and the side that did it best would win. In 1966 the improved security in a number of the CAP villages indicated some of the CAPs were doing this well.

> The CAPs were frequently required to participate in joint operations with ARVN or US forces, and this took away from the time they had to accomplish their primary counterinsurgency missions in the villages. The rationale for having the CAPs participate in large operations may have been that the CAPs knew the areas of their villages well, or that they were familiar with the people in the area. On occasions, though, the CAPs were required to participate in operations in areas away from their villages, meaning that at times they were simply used as an additional infantry force. As a result of having to take part in large operations all day, the CAP members were tired when they needed to conduct their patrols and ambushes at night. Also, they had little time to plan their activities and to prepare their equipment. A more subtle negative effect of having the CAPs leave the villages to take part in large operations was that the villagers saw thc CAPs lcavc the villages undefended.

There may or may not have been a risk involved with having the CAPs leave for one day, but it was important for the Vietnamese people to see the CAPs as a permanent security element in the villages. If the people were expected to give their loyalty to the CAPs, they needed to know the CAPs would not abandon them.[19]

Using the CAPs on operations in areas where the CAP members knew the area and the people had some merit, but usually it was a misuse of a specialized resource. The CAPs were carefully developed units intended for the difficult counterinsurgency jobs in the Vietnamese villages. Using them as an additional infantry force on an operation was similar to using a scalpel for a job more appropriate for a hammer. An additional risk in doing this was that the CAPs might have men killed or wounded on these operations, and the casualties among the CAP members could not be easily replaced with qualified men. Because the CAPs were ordered to participate in these operations frequently, it implies the Marine Corps either did not place a high priority on the mission of the CAPs, or the Marine Corps was not able to control how the CAPs were used by infantry units. Regardless of why this was the case, the effect was that it hindered the ability of the CAPs to conduct their counterinsurgency work in the villages, and it probably caused the Vietnamese people to wonder whether they could count on the CAPs to defend them.

One of the primary jobs of the Marines in the CAPs was to train the PFs, and the Marines were doing this in their own way. Officially, formal classes for the PFs were supposed to be conducted by the Marines, but little formal training was actually done in the CAPs. The PFs were part-time soldiers, and when they were not involved in the military activities of the CAPs many of them had to work to support their families. After they were on patrols and ambushes most of the night, few of the PFs wanted to sit in classes conducted by Marines who were often younger and less experienced in combat than they were. The real improvement in the military capabilities of the PFs took place on a more informal basis when the Marines and the PFs worked together in the CAPs.[20]

Adding a squad of Marines to the PF platoons in the villages generally increased the morale and the self-confidence of the PFs considerably. The Marines were motivated, well-armed, and confident they could defeat the guerrillas, and they were usually able to use US artillery, air, and reaction forces to support the CAPs when they were in a battle. After the CAPs defeated the guerrillas in a few fights, the PFs began to believe the combined force could be victorious. Because the CAPs performed as stronger and more proficient fighting units than the PF platoons had performed by themselves, the morale and the self-confidence of the PFs was improved.

As they conducted military operations with the Marines, the PFs began to adopt their discipline and their military techniques. This was partly because the Marines insisted on it, but the PFs also did this because their survival depended on it, and their pride made many of them want to do as well as the Marines. The Marines did train the PFs to clean their weapons regularly, and they trained them in marksmanship, but this was not done in a classroom setting. The Marines were training the PFs to be better fighters, but it was being accomplished more through example than through teaching in a formal classroom setting.[21]

Even though the Marines trained the PFs, the performance of the PFs was uneven, but it was necessary to have the PFs in the CAPs. One reason for this was that the Marines could train the PFs and improve their morale, but in the end, it was up to the Vietnamese to either win or lose the war. In his book, *Learning to Eat Soup With a Knife*, John Nagl made the point that, "On their own, foreign forces cannot defeat an insurgency; the best they can hope for is to create the conditions that will enable local forces to win it for them."[22] In a variation of this, the CAPs were able to create the conditions needed for the PFs to win the counterinsurgency war by bringing together the strength of the Marines' fighting ability with the PFs' strengths of their local knowledge and their cultural connections with the people. With the PFs in these hybrid units the possibility of the CAPs defeating the NLF guerrillas was greatly improved.

After securing the village against the guerrillas, the most important job of the CAPs was to gather intelligence, and many of the CAPs were doing this well. With increased security the villagers had more money because the NLF tax collectors were no longer able to come to the villages, and the guerrillas could no longer come into the villages to take recruits for their army and food for their soldiers. In contrast to the guerrillas, the Marines and the PFs took nothing from the people. Instead, they gave them protection, help, and friendship. Partly for these reasons, the people were living a better life in the villages because of the presence of the CAPs, and many of them were willing to provide the CAPs with intelligence. The people usually gave the intelligence to the PFs who gave the information to the Marines, and the Marines then passed the intelligence to their headquarters. The role the CAPs played in gathering this intelligence was crucial because it is unlikely the Vietnamese villagers would have directly given this intelligence information to ARVN forces or US infantry units.

Various intelligence agencies that were familiar with the areas where the CAPs were located confirmed the value of their intelligence. The majority of the agencies reported specific instances when the intelligence provided by the CAPs was useful for their operations. A number of commanders thought so highly of the intelligence-gathering operation of the CAPs that they said it was the greatest contribution the CAPs made to the war.[23]

The civic action the Marines did in the villages was intended to be a part of the total CAP effort to help improve the lives of the people so that they would prefer the lives they were actually living to the promised changes the NLF offered. The Marines were doing some civic action work, but they were limited in how much of this they could do. Small civic action projects took little time to complete, and many of the people appreciated the real benefits these projects provided. Examples of these small projects were teaching children to swim, teaching athletics, and encouraging village cleanups.[24] Among these projects were some which helped the people economically, such as convincing people to plant an additional vegetable crop out of the traditional season, digging wells, and improving irrigation systems for the rice paddies.

These small civic action projects often helped improve life for the people, but the most popular civic action project among the villagers was the medical assistance they received from the Navy corpsmen in the CAPs. A Marine who served in a CAP said when the corpsman had sick call, "Sometimes over a hundred peasants showed up." He thought the corpsman's work was so valuable that "You won't find too many Marines that'll dispute the fact that Doc won more hearts and minds than all of us combined."[25] The corpsmen were available to treat the Vietnamese almost every day, and this medical care did more to create good relations between the CAPs and the people than almost any other CAP activity.

The psychological operations the CAPs conducted were simple, but they worked well. In the first CAPs formed in the Phu Bai area, the Marines and the PFs spread information about CAP victories, and they told the people these victories showed the CAPs were winning the war in the villages. The CAP members also made sure all the people knew about the civic action projects which made life in the villages better. These were basic psychological operations the first CAPs performed to convince the people the guerrillas could not win, and that life in the villages was better than it would be with the guerrillas in control. As the CAP program expanded, many of the new CAPs continued to use simple but effective psychological operations such as these in an attempt to gain the loyalty of the Vietnamese people for the CAPs.

Both the civic action projects and the psychological operations some of the CAPs initiated were simple and effective. The small civic action projects were effective because they created meaningful benefits for the people in a relatively short period of time, and making these improvements helped to forge a closer relationship between the CAP members and the villagers. The psychological operations of the CAPs were effective because they were based on real victories over the guerrillas, and real improvements in the lives of the people. The villagers could quickly confirm on their own whether the CAPs defeated the guerrillas, and they could see any improvements in the village. These limited civic action and psychological operations worked well as counterinsurgency measures for the CAPs because they were based on facts the people knew were true.

To some extent the Marines in the CAPs worked to strengthen local government and local institutions in the villages, but the wisest course of action was usually to allow these institutions to work as they had in the past. In the village the council of elders controlled the traditional form of local government, and the Marines learned to work with the local government, and not to attempt to change it. In any event, advice given the council of elders by young Marines probably would not have been well-received. In most respects this was true for the local institutions in the Vietnamese villages, as well. The PF platoon was a local institution that was an exception to this, and the Marines helped make the PFs a respected fighting force that fulfilled its function of defending the villages.[26]

One mission the CAPs were given was to help the central GVN government improve its control over the villages, and events beyond their control inhibited the CAPs from helping with this. The men in the CAPs gained the loyalty of some of the Vietnamese people because they provided security for the village, they accomplished civic action projects, they took nothing from the people, and they generally treated the people well. The people could easily see, though, that the benefits they derived from the presence of the CAPs came almost exclusively from the United States, and not from the GVN. The people saw security in the villages improve when the Marines helped the local PF platoons defend the villages, but any outside supplies used in civic action projects came from US resources. Also, the popular medical programs were performed by US Navy corpsmen and not GVN medics.

If GVN control of the villages were to be extended over the villages in a beneficial manner, GVN personnel and resources needed to be used. Attempts were made to encourage more GVN involvement in the CAP program, but the GVN was either unable or unwilling to do this.[27] Because the GVN did not capitalize on the successes of the CAPs, it missed an opportunity to increase its popularity among the Vietnamese people, and to increase its control over the villages.

A Summary of CAP Counterinsurgency Task Performance in 1966

In 1966 the CAP program was beginning to demonstrate that the CAPs were capable of accomplishing most of the counterinsurgency tasks they needed to be successful. The counterinsurgency goal of security for the villages was being achieved as the CAPs defeated the guerrillas and kept them away from the people. The people were the true prize, and by keeping the NLF away from the people the CAPs kept the guerrillas away from the source of the supplies, the recruits, and the intelligence they needed. As far as the vital task of gathering intelligence was concerned, the intelligence operations of the CAPs were praised by US intelligence agencies to the extent that they said the CAPs were some of their best sources of intelligence information. With their limited resources some CAPs were also conducting basic but adequate civic action and psychological operations in many of the villages. In regard to strengthening local government, most of the Marines in the CAPs wisely allowed the local governments to operate as they operated in the past, and this was true for most of the local institutions, also. However, the Marines did improve the local institution of the PF militia in most villages. Despite these counterinsurgency successes, there were problems which kept the CAPs from operating to their full potential as a counterinsurgency concept.

The CAPs experienced some difficulties in performing their counterinsurgency work in the villages, but most of their problems were beyond their control. The best possible volunteers were needed by the CAPs for their complicated and dangerous missions, but it was hard to get these volunteers from the infantry units. The infantry was not only being asked to send men it needed to the CAPs; it was being asked to send its best men. To compound this problem, the Marine Corps was not allocated additional manpower quotas to compensate for the men sent to the CAPs. Frequently the CAPs were not given the supplies they needed to do their work well. On many occasions they did not have enough food, weapons, radios, and other supplies. Temporary shortages are understandable, but this was a recurring problem. Help with the civic action projects and the psychological operations could have also come from GVN sources, and this might have helped the GVN create and strengthen a favorable image of itself in the villages. For various reasons, though, the GVN did not do this.

It is surprising that a concept with as much apparent potential as the CAP program received so little support during this period of the Vietnam War. The strategy and the tactics of the NLF and the NVA were confusing for US commanders, though, and there were many different ideas with apparent potential as to how the war should be fought. Many of the people who had these ideas were insisting their ideas be made a priority, and they were competing to have resources assigned to their programs. The CAP program was only one among many, and Westmoreland was among those who did not think the CAP concept was that promising. Regardless, it is hard to imagine why additional men and more supplies could not have been found to help the CAPs with the counterinsurgency war. As it was, the responsibility was given almost exclusively to understrength and poorly supplied squads of Marines and platoons of PFs.

One of the greatest problems for the entire war effort for the US and its allies was the alienation of the Saigon government from most of the Vietnamese people. A Vietnamese village elder expressed much of the reason for this alienation well when he contrasted the GVN leaders with Ho Chi Minh. He said, "We are not Communists, even though we do not know exactly what a Communist is." For the village elder the problem was simpler than ideology, and he said, "But we admire and respect Ho Chi Minh. He led the struggle which threw out the foreign French. And he lives the life of a peasant." Unlike Ho Chi Minh, he said, "Our South Vietnamese generals in Saigon wear silk clothes and ride in big cars and send their wives to France and Japan for eye fixings so they can look like foreigners." In contrast to the GVN leaders he said, "Not Ho Chi Minh. He owns only two suits of clothes, wears sneakers, and rides to work on a bicycle." The village elder's conclusion was powerful and difficult to dispute when he said, "He may be a Communist. But we would like to have a leader like him around here."[28] It is difficult to imagine anything the US and its allies could have said to counter the truth in this village elder's statement.

However, there were specific instances when some of the Vietnamese people demonstrated they preferred to live in regions controlled by the CAPs. After a CAP was formed in the village of Ky Bich near Chu Lai, the people of the village began to sleep in their homes again. Before the CAP was located in the village the people moved each evening to an area three miles away to avoid the NLF guerrillas. In another situation approximately twenty-eight hundred Vietnamese moved into a hamlet near Da Nang after CAPs were established in the area. These people said they did this because they thought the CAP-controlled region was the safest place to live in the area.[29] At a minimum, these actions showed the CAP-controlled villages were acquiring a reputation as villages where the people could live away from most of the violence of the war.

Other Problems Beyond Their Control

Among the events in 1966 which negatively affected all of the pacification efforts of the Marine Corps in I Corps were the conflicts between the Saigon government and Buddhist political activists in Hue, Danang, and some of the other cities in I Corps. This conflict centered around the desire of some Buddhist factions to replace the government of Thieu and Ky with a democratically elected, civilian government in which the Buddhists could play a prominent part. The commander of ARVN forces in I Corps was Major General Nguyen Chanh Thi. Thi was popular with the troops, and he was also a devout Buddhist who shared some political views with the activists. Ky saw Thi as a political rival, and in March he removed him from command and placed him under house arrest. These actions enraged the Buddhists, and riots and demonstrations forced the government to agree to hold elections within a few months. When Ky reneged on this agreement, the Buddhists were angered by this betrayal and new rioting began. This rioting became more violent and widespread as some ARVN troops loyal to Thi joined forces with thousands of Buddhists. As the conflict escalated there were instances of open combat between ARVN soldiers loyal to the GVN and those who supported the Buddhists.

In June troops loyal to Saigon crushed the rebellion, and General Thi was placed under permanent house arrest.[30] The rebellion ended, but deep divisions within the South Vietnamese society were only made greater. On a number of occasions Walt used threats and negotiations to keep the two sides from openly fighting each other. Some Vietnamese were upset because the Marines supported the GVN in the conflict, and they resented the Marines as a result of this. Also, in the confusion created by the political crisis, NLF guerrillas were able to infiltrate areas considered pacified before the start of the disturbances.[31] After the political crisis was concluded the CAPs were faced with a situation in which they had to work harder to get the goodwill of some of the Vietnamese people, and they also faced the possibility of more guerrilla activity in the villages.

Another event with far-reaching consequences for the CAP program began in the summer of 1966 when a new front opened in the war with NVA forces infiltrating across the DMZ into the northernmost provinces of I Corps. Westmoreland thought the NVA intended to create an area where a liberation government could be established. For their part, Walt and Krulak thought the NVA was attempting to draw the Marines away from the coastal plains, and into battles in the thick jungle of the interior. Westmoreland and Walt agreed, though, that the threat needed to be met, and Marines were sent to find the NVA forces. After a series of hard fights, the NVA withdrew, but the threat that they might return remained. Because of this the Marines stationed more troops closer to the DMZ to deal with any future incursions by the NVA.[32]

The NVA incursions below the DMZ were calculated to draw Marine forces away from their successful pacification work among the people in the coastal region of I Corps. Walt and Krulak's suspicions that the NVA incursions were an attempt to draw the Marines away from the populated coastal areas and into battles in the interior were substantiated by DRV leaders. A prominent member of the DRV government said their plan was to "Entice the Americans close to the North Vietnamese border and will bleed them without mercy. In South Vietnam, the pacification program will be destroyed."[33] In 1967 Giap wrote an article for the DRV armed forces newspaper, *Quang Doi Nhan Dan*, in which he stated the NVA lured the Marines into battles at the DMZ to take the Marines away from their pacification work in the coastal areas.[34] Many of the Marine units sent to the DMZ region were taken from the populated coastal area where they were conducting and supporting pacification programs. These statements show the populated coastal areas of I Corps were vitally important to the NLF, and they wanted to disrupt the pacification programs because they were too successful.

Toward the end of 1966 the CAP program was having success as a counterinsurgency concept in the Vietnam War, but greater success was frustrated by matters beyond the control of the CAPs. The CAPs were accomplishing the primary counterinsurgency job of security for the villages, and they were working well with the PFs. There was always the problem of having too few Marines for the CAPs, and this problem was only increased when the Marine infantry units were sent to the DMZ to fight the NVA. For those battles the infantry needed every man they had, and they were understandably reluctant to send men to the CAPs. The CAPs were not supplied well enough, but they worked well with what they were given. In the field of intelligence, the CAPs did a superb job, and they were acquiring a reputation as a source of good intelligence information. The CAP civic action and psychological operations were succeeding with their fundamental techniques. As far as strengthening the loyalty of the village to the central government was concerned, the GVN could have taken over the operation of civic action programs the CAPs started, but this was not done. Despite these problems, the CAP program was generally doing well as a counterinsurgency tactic at this time in the war, but it would have performed in a better manner with more support.

However, the war was crushing in its violence, and some Vietnamese were overwhelmed by the inept and destructive manner in which it was being fought. A disillusioned ARVN officer said, "The insensitivity and ill-conceived policies of the men at the top, Saigon generals and American officials alike, were turning many of the people in the cities, and even some in the Vietnamese Army, against them." As a result of the war the officer said, "Our entire country was being devastated by fire, iron, and chemicals. People and soldiers continued to die for causes (freedom, justice, social and economic equity) that they heard a lot about, but never enjoyed. Many of those who weren't killed or wounded lived in suffering and misery."[35] This officer described the war the GVN and the Americans were fighting as hypocritical and brutal. At this time in the war the CAPs were working to protect the villagers from the worst violence of the war. The CAP program was only a small part of the US war effort, though. Whether the CAPs could play a larger role in the war was still to be seen.

Chapter 5

Combined Action Platoon Pacification and the Phong Bac Experiment

During 1966 the CAP program was having some problems, but it was also having some success as a counterinsurgency concept. Generally, the CAPs were accomplishing the basic counterinsurgency tasks of securing the villages, gathering intelligence, performing civic action, and performing psychological operations. Many of the problems the CAPs were having in accomplishing their counterinsurgency tasks during 1966 were a result of a lack of support for the program. The CAPs were not able to assist in strengthening the loyalty of the local people for the GVN because the GVN exhibited little if any interest in doing this. Despite this lack of support, the CAPs were showing promise in their counterinsurgency work at this point in the war.

Continued Criticism and Faint Vindication

In 1966 some officials in the US government were criticizing the Marine Corps for not being more aggressive. Understandably, these officials wanted to win the war as soon as possible, and Westmoreland's attrition strategy and search and destroy tactics were promoted as a fast way to defeat the enemy. In I Corps the Marine Corps was using the classic counterinsurgency strategy of slowly expanding enclaves and pacifying the areas within the enclaves. In contrast to the strategy of attrition and the tactics of search and destroy, this approach was seen as lacking fast results. Robert McNamara was one of these critical officials, and when Victor Krulak met with him in May 1966 Krulak thought McNamara questioned the progress the Marine Corps was making in the war. Krulak was frustrated by McNamara's comments, and he responded with a letter explaining what the Marine Corps had accomplished, and why he thought its strategy and the tactics were appropriate.

Krulak began by saying the Marines were fighting the war as they were partly because "The enemy, the terrain and the mission all unite to dictate the tactics."[1] He said the NLF main force units in the mountainous areas beyond the populated coastal region were of little immediate importance because they did not present much of a threat. However, he said if these units could be definitely located and attacked in situations advantageous to the Marines, then this should be done. Doing this destroyed the strength of the main force units, and it kept them from massing for attacks on Marine positions, but he did not think the Marines should be pursuing these NLF units simply to enlarge body counts of NLF dead. This was in keeping with his criticism of the strategy of attrition favored by Westmoreland and some others. Krulak made the central point that the Marines were primarily engaged in pacification in their areas of responsibility, and this, he stated, was the principal mission of the war. Krulak stressed, "The battle itself has to be fought in terms of weeding the guerrillas out of the villagers' lives, and thus breaking the nexus between Hanoi and its target—the people of South Vietnam." He said the Marines were eliminating the guerrillas in the villages, and then securing these villages so the guerrillas could not return. Part of this pacification process was the training of local militias to help in the defense of the secured villages. The slow, methodical pacification and defense of an increasingly larger enclave was the most important mission for winning the war, in Krulak's opinion. He supported his thinking by saying intelligence sources confirmed North Vietnamese leaders recently stated the survival of the guerrilla movement in South Vietnam was one of their most critical concerns.

In the conclusion of his letter to McNamara, Krulak said the Marines were fighting in a way to address all the problems of the war, and not part of those problems. If pacification of the populated areas were not made the primary mission of the war the guerrillas would continue to control the people of the country, and the guerrillas depended on the people to give them the food, recruits, and intelligence they needed. He continued to see the control of the population as the key to winning the counterinsurgency war in South Vietnam. The progress in pacification activities in I Corps was difficult to measure, he thought, but he saw pacification as the most important mission.[2]

The pressure on the Marine Corps must have been intense during this period, because in July 1966 Krulak wrote another letter in response to Secretary of the Navy Paul H. Nitze's criticism of the performance of the Marine Corps in South Vietnam. Nitze told Krulak the Marines were not moving at a fast enough offensive pace, they were not pursuing large operations enough, and they were not carrying an adequate share of the burden in the war. In his response Krulak stated the Marines were, in fact, contributing more than their share to the war, and he said, "To criticize the fundamental structure of the Marine operations is to place an incorrect interpretation on what really constitutes progress in the conflict." In the letter Krulak suggested the

Marine Corps was fighting the war in a more effective way than the US Army.[3]

Krulak used facts to show the Marine Corps was conducting more than its share of large operations in the war. He said the Marines had 28 percent of the maneuver battalions in the Free World forces in Vietnam, and they conducted 39 percent of the operations conducted by battalion size or greater forces since the beginning of 1966. Krulak then went on to say that while the Marines were doing more than their share with the large operations, the large unit operations were not as important as the other Marine efforts.

In his letter Krulak responded to Nitze's criticism with a strong argument for the enclave strategy the Marines were employing in I Corps. He discussed the counter-guerrilla operations the Marines were conducting, and why they were so important. He said these operations were important because I Corps covered approximately 27,000 square kilometers, and the coastal plain in I Corps was approximately 7,000 square kilometers. The coastal plain produced all the salt and all the fish in I Corps, and almost all of the 470,000 tons of rice produced in this region. He said the other four-fifths of I Corps were sparsely inhabited, generally inaccessible, and barely able to produce enough food to support the few tribal people who lived in the area. The 20,000 NLF and NVA troops in I Corps were located outside the coastal plains, and they needed vast amounts of rice each month to feed themselves, and because there was little food where they were located, most of the rice these troops needed had to come from the rice fields of the coastal plains, and the guerrillas made this possible.

Krulak stressed the point that the guerrillas were the vital connection between the population and the NLF and NVA main force units. He said the guerrillas got rice, collected taxes, received intelligence, and got recruits from the people, as well as spreading propaganda. Because the guerrillas knew the area and had local connections, their efforts were a necessary link in the operations of the NLF and the NVA. Krulak stated the simple but important fact that regardless of how well-equipped or well-armed the NLF and the NVA were, they could not fight without rice. He said, "Mr. McNamara rightly has said that the war will end when the enemy in South Vietnam loses his morale and his will to fight. One way to bring this about is to starve him."[4]

Krulak said the Marines were making extensive efforts to destroy the guerrillas, and because of its importance, they were trying to prevent rice from getting to the NLF and the NVA main force units. He said the counter-guerrilla campaign was of massive proportions, and it was intended to systematically eliminate the guerrillas in the area and in his opinion guerrilla casualties could not be easily replaced.

Although he did not mention the CAPs specifically, Krulak said the Vietnamese authorities showed increasing confidence in the Marines because they were giving them more control of the local forces. He said the number of PFs working with the Marines increased to the equivalent of thirty-seven platoons, and the Marines were training them to be better able to defend their villages.[5]

The detailed responses Krulak wrote to the criticism of both McNamara and Nitze show Krulak was adamantly trying to defend the performance of the Marine Corps, and to gain support for a strategy he thought would win the war. The complaints expressed regarding Marine Corps activities indicate these highly placed officials were convinced Westmoreland's strategy of attrition would bring a fast conclusion to the war. They did not want to discuss a slow enclave strategy and methodical pacification tactics. The US was impatient to win, and Krulak's protest was lost in the clamor for a quick victory.

The CAP program remained caught up in the dispute over strategy in 1966 because of the attitudes of officials such as

McNamara and Nitze. The US Army disliked the Marine Corps enclave strategy, and the US Army specifically said it would not give the Marine Corps additional personnel quotas for the CAP program. With the secretary of defense and the secretary of the navy pressuring the Marine Corps to perform in a manner more in keeping with the strategy of attrition, there was little chance of gaining support from them for the enclave strategy and the CAP program. Regardless of how well the CAPs did as a counterinsurgency concept, they were not seen by many high officials as a promising way to help win the war.

In 1966, though, a study was completed that vindicated much of what the Marine Corps was doing with the enclave strategy and pacification. US Army Chief of Staff Harold K. Johnson disagreed with Westmoreland's approach, and he commissioned a study conducted by US Army officers to examine other approaches which might be more successful. The completed *Program for the Pacification and Long-Term Development of South Vietnam* (PROVN) study rejected the strategy of attrition and the tactics of search and destroy, and said the focus of the war should be placed on pacification. The current strategy was not working, the study stated, and it could not work because it was having no effect on the NLF guerrilla organization. A necessary change in tactics for pacification meant "Security forces must be associated and intermingled with the people on a long-term basis. Their capacity to establish and maintain public order and stability must be physically and continuously credible." The study stressed, "The key to achieving such security lies in the conduct of effective area saturation tactics, in and around populated areas, which deny VC encroachment opportunities." The loyalty of the people was the true prize in the war, and "the critical actions are those that occur at the village, district, and provincial levels. This is where the war must be fought; this is where that war and the object which lies beyond it must be won." The study emphasized a change in strategy that focused on pacification was not simply a good idea for consideration. Instead, it said a focus on pacification was vitally necessary because "The situation in South Vietnam has seriously deteriorated. 1966 may well be the last chance to ensure eventual success."[6] The US Army officers who conducted the study could hardly have been more forceful in urging the adoption of the changes they proposed in the PROVN study.

Ironically, at the time the study was completed many of the recommendations in the PROVN study were already an integral part of the enclave strategy and the CAP program. Much of the thinking in the PROVN study was reflected in Krulak's two previously submitted strategic proposals, his letter to McNamara, and his letter to Nitze. Krulak repeatedly said the strategy of attrition and the tactics of search and destroy were futile, and they could not be successful in defeating the NLF and the NVA. The slowly expanding enclaves were intended to pacify the highly populated coastal areas. That is, the purpose of the enclave strategy was "The conduct of effective area saturation tactics, in and around populated areas, which deny VC encroachment opportunities." Part of the protection of the populated areas proposed in PROVN for the populated areas was accomplished by the CAPs in the enclaves. The CAPs lived in the villages and protected them from NLF infiltration, and they were the security forces which "Must be associated and intermingled with the people on a long-term basis." Part of the mission and the actions of the CAPs could be described by saying, "Their capacity to establish and maintain public order and stability must be physically and continuously credible." The manifestation of many of the conclusions of the PROVN study in the strategy and the tactics that the Marine Corps was employing in I Corps was striking. The similarity in the PROVN study's conclusion to Krulak's thinking was striking, also. In keeping with the final conclusion of PROVN, Krulak stated on various occasions that the primary use of the strategy of attrition and the tactics of search and destroy in the war would result in a loss for the United States.

Eventually PROVN was sent to Westmoreland who was understandably critical of the study. The conclusions in PROVN were a direct challenge to Westmoreland's authority, and to the strategy and the tactics he chose to fight the war. He saw problems with PROVN because "It must be realized that there are substantial difficulties and dangers inherent in implementing this or any similar program.... Any major reorganization such as envisioned by PROVN must be phased and deliberate to avoid confusion and slow-down in ongoing programs." To lessen any impact the study might have Westmoreland determined the study should be a "conceptual document" for further study.[7] In this way, Westmoreland blocked the possibility that the changes proposed by PROVN could result in a more effective US strategy and more effective tactics for the Vietnam War.

Lt. Col. William R. Corson and Phong Bac

One of the most intriguing people in the history of the CAPs was US Marine Corps Lieutenant Colonel William R. Corson, who was placed in charge of the CAP program in February 1967. Corson was both capable and brilliant, but he was also irascible and outspoken to a fault. In 1942 Corson had joined the Marine Corps after he left the University of Chicago where he was studying math and physics on a scholarship. After fighting in the Pacific as an enlisted man during World War II, Corson returned to the University of Chicago where he earned a degree in math. When he completed his degree, Corson reenlisted in the Marine Corps and received a commission as an officer. Later Corson earned a doctorate in economics from American University. Soon after he reenlisted in the Marine Corps Corson began working with the Central Intelligence Agency (CIA) on projects which were primarily in Asia, and he eventually learned to speak fluent Chinese. During this period of his career he became an expert in insurgency warfare which he said he learned about and practiced in "Viet Nam, in Indonesia, Thailand, China and a few other unmentionable places. That's been my profession." In 1966 Corson was teaching Chinese communist military tactics at the US Naval Academy when he was asked to return to South Vietnam.[8]

When Corson arrived in South Vietnam in September 1966, he was given command of the Third Tank Battalion of the Third Marine Division located approximately nine miles southwest of Danang. Considering Corson's experience in Asia and his expertise in counterinsurgency warfare, it is not realistic to think he was brought to South Vietnam to command a tank battalion. It was Lewis Walt who asked Corson to come to South Vietnam, and this was the period during which Walt and Krulak decided to expand the CAP program. Because of his experience and his ability Corson was a natural fit to command the expansion, and it is likely Walt had this in mind when he requested Corson. The possibility this was the case became more of a probability when Corson began an experimental pacification program in the hamlet of Phong Bac soon after he arrived at his new command.

Corson later said the pacification program experiment he initiated at Phong Bac was important for the CAP program because it was a test case for the CAPs. Corson probably knew he would be taking command of the CAP program, and he probably knew the CAPs were intended to work as small units to pacify the Vietnamese villages. Later he said he took the successful techniques developed in the experimental program at Phong Bac and taught them to the Marines in the CAP program.[9]

The Third Tank Battalion was stationed in the area of Phong Bac and performed some of the standard US civic action activities before Corson took command. Among these activities were passing out candy and toys to the children, distributing soap, and giving the people food supplies. In Corson's opinion, these activities were done out of a sense of compassion for the poverty of the people, but it was also assumed gratitude for these actions would somehow turn the people against the NLF.

The attitude of the Marines quickly changed when a Marine position was attacked by the NLF and the Marines suffered a number of casualties. The Vietnamese civilians gave no warning of the attack, although it was suspected they had knowledge of it. Additionally, a Regional Forces camp located close to the attacked Marine position did not attempt to help the Marines during the attack. The Marines thought the Vietnamese civilians and the Regional Forces were ungrateful after the Marines were generous with the Vietnamese civilians, and they felt betrayed. Because of the hostility the Marines felt toward the Vietnamese, they withdrew into their camp as if it were a fortress, and they had little contact with either the civilians or the Regional Forces. In a pattern that was common among US military units in the war after similar incidents, the Marines concentrated on conventional military actions against the NLF and ignored civic action.[10]

The most difficult problem the US military faced in South Vietnam, in Corson's opinion, was pacification, and this was critical because successful pacification was necessary if the war were to be won. He said, "Of all the tasks the military has been confronted with in Vietnam pacification has been the most troublesome and complex." He looked at previous pacification programs the US used in South Vietnam, and he tried to see why they failed. One reason he saw was that the GVN officials in charge of many of them had little interest in seeing the programs succeed. The American-initiated programs such as plans for popular elections, land reform, and the elimination of corruption would destroy cultural practices established over centuries, and these practices were the basis for the wealth and the position of the officials. The responsibility of these officials was to the people who put them in their positions, and not to the Americans. They felt safe to do as they wished because US military power would protect them, regardless of what they did. Also, pacification programs failed because the ARVN either would not or could not keep the guerrillas away from areas the ARVN was trying to pacify. Part of the reason for these ARVN failures, Corson thought, was that the ARVN lacked good leadership, was poorly motivated, and had generally poor morale.

Corson also thought Americans assumed they knew what the Vietnamese people wanted instead of finding out what they truly wanted. After the US built schools and bridges for the people because it was assumed this is what they wanted, the error was compounded by thinking the people would support the GVN and oppose the NLF in gratitude for the new projects. Two of the conclusions Corson drew regarding pacification were that the US was at the mercy of the GVN in past pacification programs, and the culture and the conditions in South Vietnam that caused the failure of pacification were not changed.

Corson thought the base of the pacification question was how to counter the ideological appeal of the NLF. The NLF received support from the people, he thought, because they were Vietnamese from their hamlets, or from hamlets like theirs. Also, the NLF fought the traditional enemies of the people who were the wealthy people of the cities, the absentee landlords, the corrupt landlords, and foreign invaders, such as the Americans. While many Vietnamese disliked the NLF practices of taking their young men to be guerrillas and charging high taxes, they clung to the hope an NLF victory would bring a better life for themselves. However, even though the people felt a strong emotional appeal for the NLF, they feared hunger more.

Once he took over the program, a unique method Corson used to establish a rapport between the Marines and the Vietnamese was the game of *co tuong* which is similar to chess and is played throughout much of Asia. Corson knew how to play *co tuong*, and he also knew the game was played by virtually everyone in Vietnamese society. After he taught some of his Marines to play the game, Corson organized a *co tuong* tournament in the village with a transistor radio as the prize for the winner. The tournament was well-attended, and the eventual winner was a hamlet chief. After the tournament ended Corson challenged the hamlet chief to a game of *co tuong*, and the game ended in a draw. In the days following the tournament the Marines who knew how to play *co tuong* went into the village and played a number of games with the villagers. Playing this popular game together helped the Marines and the Vietnamese to get to know each other, and a number of friendships resulted from this.[11]

After the tournament Corson began to go into the village to play *co tuong* with one of the village elders. The village elder knew Chinese, and he and Corson spoke in Chinese while they played the game. As they played, Corson eventually began to tactfully ask the village elder about the beliefs, the desires, and the fears of the people in the village. The man was open with Corson, and as a result of their conversations Corson came to the conclusion that showing the people how to end their fear of hunger by helping them become economically independent was the best way to approach pacification in Phong Bac.[12]

The pacification program Corson put into practice did not rely on the GVN or the ARVN for its success, but instead it relied on the Marines, and went directly to the Vietnamese people as its objcctive. As the program was conducted, the Marines protected the village to prevent NLF interference. Corson said, "I believed that my program should not depend upon the Vietnamese military for its successful implementation." Instead, Corson concluded, "The decision, therefore, was to go it alone, relying on the Marines, and to deal directly with the end object of pacification—the peasant." The emotional support for the NLF was ignored, and Corson chose to emphasize the desire of the people to make money. The people could still think they were loyal to the nationalism of the NLF, but they also wanted to make money to avoid poverty and starvation. To do this the Marines suggested projects to make money, and they let the people and a village business council decide which projects should be adopted. The Marines helped by providing their labor and technical help with projects such as pig farms and rabbit farms, but the people of the village decided which projects they wanted. After a period of time the people began to make money, and this economic success gave them a sense of security and hope. In this way the Marines used the resources of the area to show the people how to acquire money for themselves, and no US economic help was used or needed.[13]

As the people started to make money, the NLF used propaganda to attack the American-initiated economic programs. Their propaganda did not have any appeal that could overcome the fact that the people were achieving some degree of economic independence, though. The will to avoid hunger and starvation was too strong among the villagers, and the propaganda of the Marines countered by saying the NLF were bandits who stole. When the guerrillas offered bounties for the killing of the Marines, the people were shrewd enough to realize any bounty money paid would have to initially be taken from the people by the NLF. The hope of financial security countered the ideological appeal of the NLF, and Corson said in any choice between ideology and gain the people would always choose gain.

One aspect of this propaganda war between the NLF and the Marines showed the particular flair Corson acquired in his Asian experiences which helped him accomplish this mission. When the NLF criticized the economic programs the Marines helped to start in the village, Corson challenged the guerrillas to a debate in the village during the Christmas truce. The topic of the debate was to be what sort of material advantages the NLF could bring to the village, and Corson said he would come to the debate by himself if anyone from the NLF would debate him. On the day of the debate there were NLF members in the audience, but none of them chose to debate Corson. Because of this, Corson took the opportunity to discuss other business projects with which the Marines could help the village. The NLF thought they lost face when they did not debate Corson, and that evening they used loudspeakers to criticize the Marines and the business projects the Marines helped to start. Corson was aware that Asians appreciated the use of colorful and earthy insults, and he responded to the NLF propaganda by calling them "suckers of rotten turtle eggs." Some of the villagers found this amusing because this was a degrading insult made in a particularly Asian manner, and few people openly insulted the NLF.[14]

After his experiment in pacification in Phong Bac, Corson concluded that even though the GVN could not be counted on to give up its power to accomplish the pacification aims of the US, the Marines could accomplish pacification by using their own resources. He thought pacification in Phong Bac was successful because of three basic points which could be duplicated in other geographical areas. First, the Marines needed to prove they were credible by fighting and defeating the NLF. Next, they needed to have technical skills to help the people with the economic projects in the villages. Lastly, the first two elements needed to be brought together to demonstrate that the Marines could defend the people and help them build the economic projects to improve the life in the villages.

A Vietnamese Perspective of the Phong Bac Experiment

A fascinating Vietnamese perspective on Corson's pacification project in Phong Bac was obtained by the author William J. Lederer while he was doing research in South Vietnam during 1967. Lederer did not know about the Phong Bac project at the time, and he did not know Corson. He became curious, though, when a Pan American Airways official he knew told him two Vietnamese men from a hamlet called Phong Bac were in Saigon to take delivery of a number of hogs of a special breed which were flown to South Vietnam from the US. The official told Lederer the hogs and their transportation costs were paid for by the people of Phong Bac in a private business transaction, and there was no US or GVN government involvement in the venture. Lederer was intrigued by the situation, and he decided to talk with the two Vietnamese men.

The two men were reluctant to speak with Lederer at first, but when they found out he was not affiliated with either the US government or the GVN they spoke openly with him. They said Phong Bac bought the hogs because a Marine sergeant named Smith told them hogs of this breed would be the best breed to raise in the Phong Bac environment. When Lederer asked the men about Sergeant Smith, they said Colonel Corson brought Smith to them to help them with their hog-raising efforts. Lederer then asked them who Corson was, and they said he was the Marine officer who came to Phong Bac in September 1966, and who left Phong Bac a few months prior to their trip to Saigon to get the hogs. The two Vietnamese then spoke with Lederer about their experiences with Corson in Phong Bac.[15]

They said Phong Bac was a small hamlet close to Danang where the people made a living by farming rice. Doing this was difficult because most of the land in the area was owned by absentee landlords who charged the farmers 50 percent of their crop to use the land. This was twice the legal limit which was supposed to be charged for the use of the farm land, but the people were able to make a modest living. The war caused additional hardships for the hamlet though, because some villages were destroyed in the violence and many refugees from the destroyed villages came to Phong Bac. The Vietnamese told Lederer approximately fifteen hundred refugees came to Phong Bac in the previous year, and this placed a severe strain on the resources of the hamlet.

When the Marines came to Phong Bac to pacify the hamlet the people did not like them, the men told Lederer. This was partly because they saw the Americans in general as responsible for destroying villages and making refugees of many Vietnamese. Also, when American and ARVN troops came to pacify the villages the landlords came with them, and the landlords used the troops to collect rent and to mistreat them. The Marines who came to Phong Bac made the people feel as if they were beggars because "They would go through the streets giving everyone chewing gum, cigarettes, candy, things to eat, and toys to the children." The men said it is a terrible insult in Vietnamese society to be called a beggar, and when the Marines passed out free food and cigarettes these actions made the people resent them. The men confirmed Corson's assessment of Vietnamese attitudes and showed that he was on the correct track to discontinue the practice.[16]

After the Marines' camp was attacked by the guerrillas the Marines were angry with the people because none of them had warned the Marines of the impending attack. As the Marines suspected, many knew the guerrillas would attack, but they felt they had no reason to warn the Marines. The men told Lederer the villagers also did not warn the Marines because the people helped the NLF. The men said, "It seemed to us that if the NLF would win, then at least the frightful conditions of this war would come to an end." It seemed right to them to support the NLF because "The NLF mostly are farmers like ourselves and come from the same district." The only land reform the men knew of was a generation prior to this time when the Vietminh distributed land.

After the attack on their camp the Marines did not interact with the people, and they were only involved in performing their military missions in the area. After a period of time, though, some of the Marines began to come into the village to play *co tuong* with the Vietnamese. The people saw the Marines enjoyed the game, and the people appreciated that the Marines were no longer giving the Vietnamese food, candy, and cigarettes. Corson organized a *co tuong* tournament and, in fact, the older of the two men who spoke with Lederer was the hamlet chief who won the tournament. After the man won the tournament Corson approached him and asked if he would play a game of *co tuong* with Corson. The man was impressed that Corson knew some Vietnamese, and he played *co tuong* with him. Later Corson went to the most respected elder in the village and began playing *co tuong* with him. As the two men played, they spoke with each other in Chinese, and the villagers were impressed that Corson knew Asian languages. The man told Lederer, "His knowledge did us honor. He was the first foreigner who was familiar with our ways."[17]

The men said the Marines eventually began to hire boats from the villagers to fish in the Song Cau Do River which was close to the village. To get the fish the Marines threw dynamite into the river, and they caught a large number of fish which they then sold to the people at a very fair price. After the Marines did this on a few occasions, Corson spoke with the village elders at a public meeting and told them the river belonged to Phong Bac, and the people of the village should share in the profits from the sale of the fish. Corson gave the hamlet chief a total of approximately one hundred and fifty dollars, and he suggested the village form a business council to decide how the money could best be spent for the benefit of the entire community. The people considered various options, and they also asked Corson for his advice.

To help the villagers Corson had some of his Marines who were fishermen and farmers talk with the Vietnamese and suggest ways the people could improve the economy of the village. The Marines told the Vietnamese about farming cooperatives in the US, and they discussed possibilities such as bee keeping, better ways of fishing, raising hogs, and raising rabbits.

The Vietnamese decided to raise hogs as their first project, and the men said, "The young Marines worked with us when we requested it. They were not like the government men who talk big but do nothing but talk. These young Marines worked with their hands and knew how to." After working at raising hogs and other projects for a few months the average worth of each family in the village increased almost ten times.[18]

The NLF became upset because the Marines were successful in helping the villagers, and the men said, "They sent messages saying that the Marines were trying to trick us." When the hamlet chief told Corson about the messages, Corson challenged the NLF to a public debate on whether the economic projects were good for Phong Bac or not, and whether or not the Marines were lying. When Corson said he would even go alone if this would get the NLF to debate him, the hamlet chief told Corson the NLF would kill him if he went by himself. Corson replied that if the NLF came to the debate then the better argument would win, and if the NLF did not come to the debate the people would know they were liars, and if Corson were killed the people would know the NLF were liars. On the day of the debate the men said, the NLF did not come to debate Corson. After this Corson called the NLF filthy names in Vietnamese, the men said, and he was very good at this. They went on to say calling enemies filthy names is traditional in Vietnamese culture and Corson "Is the first foreigner who knows how to use filthy names with skill."[19]

In the village of Phong Bac there were a number of positive changes because of the new businesses begun while Corson was there. The new businesses the hamlet business council started employed people from approximately sixty families, and some families quit farming rice because working in the new businesses was so profitable. As a result of this, the landowners needed to encourage more people to grow rice, and they reduced the rent for the land they owned by 50 percent. The men said, "Our new businesses give the village a sense of independence. What we did, we did alone, without the help of the government." Their sense of accomplishment was greater because "We do not have to pay off a district chief for licenses or for help. We feel like an independent hamlet, which is traditional in our history."[20]

The village was independent and prosperous, and because of this the village did not want trouble with the NLF, the GVN, or the Marines; the village only wanted to be neutral in the war. On one occasion the people heard the NLF was planning an attack on the airbase at Danang, and the guerrillas were going to stay overnight in an area of the village close to the hog farms. Because they did not want the hog farms to be harmed by any fighting, some of the people told Corson about the NLF plans. The men justified this by saying, "We were not betraying the NLF or acting as informers. What we did was to make sure that the hamlet property was not harmed." Even though the Marines were still in the village and the guerrillas were still in the area, neither group bothered the villagers. The Marines were able to keep the guerrillas away from the village, and "Nobody makes speech about democracy or Ho Chi Minh or General Ky. The Marines mind their business and we mind ours. We understand each other." The Marines let the people conduct their business and remain neutral.[21]

The men from Phong Bac ended their conversation with Lederer by saying some NLF fighters came back to the village since it became prosperous. Many of the guerrillas were farmers, and they said, "That's all we farmers want—a good and peaceful life." The men joked and said if Corson were given enough time the people would be making so much money in the new businesses that the guerrillas would all come home, and the fighting would end.[22]

Later, after Lederer spoke with the two men from Phong Bac, he met and interviewed Corson. In this interview Corson gave some additional information about the pacification experiment at Phong Bac. He said he developed his pacification program at

Phong Bac by studying the pacification programs the French, the Vietnamese, and the Americans attempted in Vietnam. All of these were failures and Corson decided to rely exclusively on the Marines in his command to conduct the pacification program in Phong Bac. Corson's study brought him to the conclusion that pacification needed to focus on the Vietnamese people, and to look at the process of pacification from the perspective of the people. All the pacification activities needed to take into consideration the economic and the social life of the Vietnamese people, and the people needed to decide for themselves whether or not the course of action the Marines wanted from them was best for the villagers.[23]

An Evaluation of the Phong Bac Experiment

It is revealing to look at the description of the pacification process at Phong Bac from the perspective of both Corson and the two Vietnamese men from the hamlet. By looking at Corson's description we see what he intended to do, and what he thought he accomplished. The description of Corson's actions given by the men from the hamlet shows how the villagers responded to Corson's actions, and what they thought the results of the pacification process were. Comparing the two descriptions helps to see how well Corson accomplished his objectives.

Corson's knowledge of Asian culture and his study of earlier pacification efforts helped him to develop the pacification program in Phong Bac. He saw the previous pacification attempts by the French, the Vietnamese, and the Americans did not work, and he did not think the civic action programs of the Marines would help to pacify the Vietnamese villages. This was confirmed by the men with whom Lederer spoke who said it made the people of the village feel as if they were beggars when the Marines gave them things such as food and cigarettes. Rather than encouraging them to like the Marines, these actions caused the Vietnamese to resent them. Corson knew this was true of Vietnamese culture, and he knew simply giving the people material goods would not gain their loyalty. After the villagers did not warn the Marines about the coming attack on their camp Corson realized the villagers did not like the Marines, and he looked for a way to establish a rapport with the Vietnamese.

The use of the game of *co tuong*, his Asian language skills, and his general knowledge of Asian culture also worked well for Corson. He knew from his Asian experience that knowing and playing *co tuong* would gain the respect of many of the Vietnamese. When the Marines played *co tuong* with the people, Corson thought some of the hostility between the two groups might be lessened, and he thought the *co tuong* tournament would be popular among the Vietnamese. Later, Corson showed his respect for and understanding of Vietnamese culture when he played *co toung* with the most respected elder in the village and spoke with him in Chinese. In Lederer's interview the Vietnamese men said some of the villagers were impressed when they saw a number of the Marines could play *co tuong*, and the villagers liked the *co tuong* tournament. Also, the villagers thought well of Corson because he went to the most respected elder in the village and spoke Chinese with him as they played *co tuong*. Because of this they saw Corson as someone who knew and respected their culture. The comments of these men show Corson's knowledge of Asian culture helped him to affect some rapport between the Marines and the Vietnamese people in the village.

With the Marines and the villagers at least not hostile toward each other, Corson approached the problem of how to separate the people from the NLF, and in this instance his knowledge of counterinsurgency and economics worked well for him. Corson saw the family, the community, and the cultural bonds between the people and the NLF were too strong to be broken, and his study of earlier, failed pacification programs in Vietnam helped him come to this conclusion.

A central strength of guerrilla movements is that the guerrillas only have to promise the people a better life in the future when they succeed, and they can attack existing economic and social problems which helped create the revolution. In *Isolating the Guerrilla*, Michael F. Trevett wrote, "Every insurgency situation is the result ... of popular grievances, which have led to revolt." The challenge for the counterinsurgency forces was finding a way "To offer a viable and more attractive alternative to what the guerrilla promises, and by contrast to remove some of his support."[24] Because he knew there was little chance of breaking the strong connections between the people and the NLF, Corson chose to create a better life in the present to counter the guerrillas' promise of a better life in the future. The economic program Corson conceived dealt with the primary fear of hunger among the Vietnamese villagers.

The comments of the two Vietnamese men to Lederer showed Corson chose a useful method to bring the villagers to act in a way which was beneficial for the Marines. The connections between the people and the NLF were too strong, and there was hope an NLF victory would indeed end the war and bring the better life the NLF promised, the men said. Still, the fear of hunger and starvation was stronger for the people because they were barely growing enough food to feed themselves. They welcomed and appreciated Corson's approach to them because he did not offer them charity. Instead, he offered them suggestions as to how they could better themselves economically, and he and the other Marines gave the people technical help to accomplish this. The Vietnamese men said the villagers were proud they achieved a degree of prosperity through their own resources, and they wanted to protect this new prosperity. They could still give the NLF their moral support, but they did not want the guerrillas to ruin the prosperity the people of the village created. Corson's plan worked because he helped the people realize the Vietnamese cultural ideal of the independent hamlet.

Corson's Plan and the CAPs as a Counterinsurgency Concept

The reactions of the Vietnamese villagers to Corson's plan suggest that Corson's pacification plan brought the villagers to act in a way which was beneficial for the Marines. Corson's intention was to use the successful elements of his pacification plan from Phong Bac throughout the CAP program after he assumed command. Because of this it is important to consider how well Corson's plan could work within the existing CAP units to accomplish the basic counterinsurgency functions this study stated the CAPs needed to perform to work well as a counterinsurgency method.

The basic counterinsurgency task is security, and the security the Marines provided for Phong Bac was good, but getting rid of the hidden guerilla cadres was still a major problem. Since the inception of the CAPs their greatest strength was their ability to defeat the guerrillas and to keep them out of the villages. Finding and eliminating the NLF cadres in the villages was a counterinsurgency task which was more difficult to complete. In Phong Bac the people knew the hidden guerrilla cadre members might endanger the relative neutrality the people wanted to maintain by attempting to send food and intelligence to the guerrillas. If this were done the people knew the Marines could react with force, and the village businesses would be at risk of being destroyed. Because of this the people of the villages were likely to attempt to avoid Marine violence and protect their businesses by either convincing the cadre members not to do this, or by betraying them. In any event the villagers probably would not have allowed the actions of the cadre to jeopardize their economic success. If Corson's pacification plan brought about similar attitudes and actions in other villages where the plan was put into practice, this would help to eliminate or neutralize the hidden NLF cadres in the villages to be pacified.

The Marines in Phong Bac received intelligence information related to NLF activities because the people did not want their businesses destroyed by fighting. With Corson's plan for economic development it is likely this would continue to be the case in other villages where the CAPs operated. As it was, the CAPs operating at the time were getting good intelligence through their patrolling and their informants in the villages. The economic prosperity of the villages could convince people who would otherwise be neutral to provide intelligence for their own economic self-interest. In this way intelligence gathering could be increased if Corson's plan were incorporated in the CAPs.

Corson's plan for economic assistance did a good job of accomplishing the counterinsurgency tasks of civic action, economic projects, and psychological operations in Phong Bac. Prosperity and economic independence were at the heart of Corson's pacification plan, and as the economic projects succeeded and the standard of living improved in the village, the other counterinsurgency tasks became easier to complete for the CAPs. Information regarding the improved living standards in the village was used for psychological operations to discredit the guerrillas and to attempt to gain people's loyalty. The villagers were living a good life in the present, and they were no longer willing to risk their lives for the NLF's promise of a better life in the future. It is reasonable to think all of these successes in civic action, economic projects, and psychological operations could be achieved if programs similar to Corson's pacification plan were started in other CAP villages.

The counterinsurgency task of strengthening and developing the local government was performed with Corson's plan because the local government oversaw the economic projects in the village. The business council and the cooperatives formed by the villagers helped to create the village prosperity, and they served as strong forces to counter corruption on the part of the elected hamlet and village chiefs. The business council and the cooperatives were also village institutions which helped to develop and strengthen the village government. Situations such as these would probably have occurred in the CAP villages when Corson's plan was implemented.

Corson's pacification plan made no effort to accomplish the counterinsurgency task of improving the control of the GVN over the village. In his opinion the GVN was corrupt and predatory, and he seemed to think the GVN was at least as great a threat to the villagers as the NLF, if not greater. Also, he determined that the GVN either would not or could not help in pacification. Because of this he chose to leave the GVN completely out of his pacification plan, using solely the Marines and the resources of the village. The GVN was the government of the country, though, and whether or not Corson would have been able to do this throughout the CAP program is questionable.

The success of Corson's pacification experiment in Phong Bac was impressive, but replicating it in the CAP villages presented at least one significant problem. The key to the success of the pacification program in Phong Bac was the development of economic projects that made the people prosperous, and the key to the development of the economic projects was the technical expertise of the Marines in Corson's command. Assuming many of the Marine infantrymen in the CAPs had any knowledge of skills such as hog farming, bee keeping, and raising rabbits was not realistic. There may have been a few, but if Corson's plan were to succeed in the CAP program generally, men with skills such as these would be needed in all the CAPs. The CAPs were having difficulty finding enough men for the program as it was, and making these skills an additional requirement for the Marines in the CAPs would have made finding qualified men impossible. How well Corson would do as the commander of the CAP program now remained to be seen.

CHIEF BRIEFS GENERAL – Kim Le Bat, Thuy Phy Village Chief, points out one of the 11 surveyed artillery concentration areas to Major General Lewis W. Walt, commander of the III Amphibious Force. Lieutenant Colonel W. W. Taylor (left) commanding the 3d Battalion, Fourth Marine Regiment, and assistant village chief Vang help explain the area and purpose of the surveyed fields of fire. *Photo courtesy of USMC Archives.*

Lieutenant Paul R. Ek (right) gestures towards a suspected NLF stronghold. On the left is a Vietnamese police chief, and the man in the center is an interpreter. *Photo courtesy of USMC Archives.*

JOINT ACTION COMPANY – Corporal Earl J. Suter (Lancaster, Penn.), 1st Fire Team Leader, and a Popular Forces soldier work on the construction of a bamboo barracks for the 1st squad of the Joint Action Company, which lived with the villagers of Thuy Luong, 2 miles south of Phu Bai, Vietnam. *Photo courtesy of USMC Archives.*

Charlie McMahon (left) and his buddies at Hotel 6 village, July 1968.
Photo courtesy of Charles McMahon.

Three Marines and one PF in the village of Loc Bon, then assigned as Combined Action Company – CAC – IV. The Marines are L-R Aurelio "Speedy" Gonzales (Texas) and Greg Boggs (Panama City Beach, Florida). Boggs was the radio operator for the Biet Kich platoon attached to the squad in the village. Marine on far right is Mike Letson from Chicago. The PF is Nguyen Phuoc. *Photo courtesy of Peter Nardie.*

Children from the village of Loc Bon headed to school. The school was partially supplied by donations to CAC Marines from their hometowns. The school's one teacher was under constant threat of assassination and never slept in her family hut. She spent every night in the main village guarded by the CAC Marines and PFs. *Photo courtesy of Peter Nardie.*

The main trail out of the village of Loc Bon. Note the overgrowth of the trails. In the daytime the trail was semi-darkened. At night, even with a moon, the trail was completely black. *Photo courtesy of Peter Nardie.*

A typical village fisherman in his boat on the Song Nong River. These boats were used to fish and to transport goods up and down and across the river. On various occasions the CAC used these boats to cross the river at night. *Photo courtesy of Peter Nardie.*

The trail along the Song Nong River which bisected the village of Loc Bon east to west. The village was approximately 15 km south of the major Marine base at Phu Bai. This trail followed the Song Nong River west toward the Au Shau valley. *Photo courtesy of Peter Nardie.*

Operation Golden Fleece. *Photo courtesy of USMC Archives.*

Rice harvest. Private Gary Hutchinson helps Vietnamese harvest their rice crop under the watchful eye of CPL. David P. Shiftlet, CAP 2-5-3. *Photo courtesy of USMC Archives.*

New Combined Action Platoon south of Hoi An strings barbed wire defenses. *Photo courtesy of USMC Archives.*

Raising the flag. Marines and Vietnamese Popular Force troops stand at attention as the senior PF raises his country's flag at H-9, a Combined Action Platoon located between Phu Bai and Da Nang. *Photo courtesy of USMC Archives.*

Commandant of the Marine Corps Wallace Greene (left) and Gen. William Westmoreland (right) discuss strategy while Gen. Cushman (center) listens. *Photo courtesy of USMC Archives.*

Col. Lewis B. "Chesty" Puller, 1950. *Photo courtesy of USMC Archives.*

Second Lt. Lewis B. Puller 1926. *Photo courtesy of USMC Archives.*

Lt. Gen. Victor H. Krulak. *Photo courtesy of USMC Archives.*

A Popular Force soldier from Combined Action Group – 4 cautiously searches the dense undergrowth for a wounded guerrilla his unit ambushed. *Photo courtesy of USMC Archives.*

La Kim Bat, village chief, and CPL John J. Shylo, assistant squad leader CAC 3, go over a new patrol route. *Photo courtesy of USMC Archives.*

A CAP unit heads home after a night in an ambush position or on patrol. *Photo courtesy of USMC Archives.*

A daily patrol is being organized for a Combined Action Platoon. *Photo courtesy of USMC Archives.*

One of the PFs working with the 4th Combined Action Group fires an M-79 at a suspected sniper location on the bank of the Nhung River south of Quang Tri City. *Photo courtesy of USMC Archives.*

PFC C.W. Hickman (left) and a Popular Force soldier cultivate a vegetable garden they have started in their compound in the hamlet of Xuan Hoi near Phu Bai. *Photo courtesy of USMC Archives.*

Combined Action Platoon Marines receive mail upon returning to their base village. *Photo courtesy of USMC Archives.*

Cpl. Eylen G. Locke of CAC unit 33 helps a PF, Hguyen Vang of Hoa Lac, remove the mold from a newly made brick. *Photo courtesy of USMC Archives.*

American officers and men in South Vietnam

The U.S. Government is waging an aggressive war against South Vietnam. It has spent billions of dollars and defamed the prestige and freedom-and-peace-loving traditions of the American people. It has caused the useless and pitiful deaths and maimings of thousands of American officers and men.

The U.S. Government has come to an impasse in South Vietnam. In order to evade the danger of a complete fiasco, it is venturing to spread the war, endangering your future more than ever.

The South Vietnamese people have won and will win.

The U.S. Government has been defeated and will be completely defeated.

DEMAND PEACE IN VIETNAM AND YOUR RETURN TO YOUR HOMELAND AND FAMILIES.

DEMAND THAT THE U.S. GOVERNMENT WITHDRAW ALL U.S. TROOPS AND ARMS FROM SOUTH VIETNAM AND LET THE VIETNAMESE PEOPLE SETTLE THEIR OWN AFFAIRS THEMSELVES.

REFUSE TO OBEY ALL ORDERS TO CARRY OUT MOPPING-UP OPERATIONS TO KILL THE VIETNAMESE PEOPLE OR ATTACK THEIR ARMED FORCES.

SYMPATHIZE WITH AND SUPPORT THE JUST STRUGGLE OF THE SOUTH VIETNAMESE PEOPLE.

THE SOUTH VIETHAM NATIONAL FRONT FOR LIBERATION

NLF propaganda leaflet found in Quang Tri Province in September 1967. *Photo courtesy of USMC Archives.*

Chapter 6

The Combined Action Platoons Become a Separate Command

In February 1967 Major General Herman J. Nickerson told Lieutenant Colonel William R. Corson that General Victor H. Krulak, General Lewis Walt, and he wanted Corson to take command of the CAP program as a separate command and to initiate an expansion. The three generals were impressed with how well Corson's pacification experiment worked in Phong Bac, and they wanted to use the CAPs as the primary pacification method to duplicate its success. The civic action programs the Marines were currently using as a means of pacification produced poor results, and they often created more harm than good.

Officially the GVN and the ARVN were responsible for accomplishing pacification, but the Marine generals thought the previous performance of both the GVN and ARVN proved they were either unable or unwilling to do the pacification work. In addition, both the GVN and the ARVN were riddled with corruption.

The generals decided if pacification were to be accomplished in I Corps, the Marines would have to find a way to do it themselves. Corson's success with the Phong Bac experiment made it look as if Phong Bac was a good template, and many of the CAP units were proving they worked well at performing counterinsurgency tasks. For these reasons the generals chose the CAPs as the central means for their plan to pacify the villages in I Corps, and they chose Corson to command the CAPs in its execution.

Corson said prior to this decision by Krulak, Walt, and Nickerson, the official mission of the CAPs in the Vietnamese villages was security and not pacification. Initially, Corson said, the CAPs were intended as a defense force in the rear areas to keep the guerrillas out of the villages and away from the people. Without some way to protect them, the rear areas in the Marine enclaves were vulnerable to guerrilla attack, and the Marines "Knew the security conditions behind our lines would become intolerable if combined action went down the chute." Before they could perform this counterinsurgency security mission the Marines and the PFs in the CAPs needed to show they could work successfully together as a military unit.[1]

The performance of the CAPs was followed closely because of the critical importance of their rear security mission. Eventually the Marines and the PFs showed they worked well together in the joint military units of the CAPs, and they also showed they were usually able to do well with their own resources while defending villages from larger guerrilla forces. Because of this the CAPs were considered to be a dependable force for the protection of the rear areas of the enclaves, but Corson said they were not given the official mission of pacification in the villages of the enclaves until February 1967.[2]

An important distinction is that many of the CAPs were doing a great deal of counterinsurgency pacification work in the villages before this, but their primary counterinsurgency task was to provide security in the areas of their villages. The operational plan Ek developed for the first CAP units in the Phu Bai area included pacification objectives, but the mission of these

CAPs was to prevent the guerrillas from getting into the areas within mortar range of the Marine base at Phu Bai. In 1966 Walt expanded the CAP program, and a number of the new CAPs in the Danang area were located in the villages close to the airbase at Danang.[3]

The primary function of these CAPs was to keep the guerrillas away from the airbase, but Walt also made some pacification duties part of their mission. Among these duties were collecting intelligence, civic action, and psychological operations.[4] As the Marines watched the CAPs succeed as a defense force for their rear areas, the potential to use the CAPs for pacification must have been seen as the Marines came to the decision to perform pacification in I Corps on their own. The CAPs and Corson's successful Phong Bac plan were then brought together to perform the pacification program.

As Corson prepared to assume command of the CAP program, he said the results of the Phong Bac pacification program showed there was an additional contributing factor which needed to be duplicated for successful pacification. Corson said in Phong Bac the Marines were ready to actively oppose not only the NLF, but also the GVN if either tried to destroy or corrupt their program. Because of this, he said, the people of the village were economically independent, and they were in charge of their own destinies, and these results could be duplicated in other villages.[5]

When Corson assumed command of the CAP program in 1967 the CAPs arguably became the most important element of the Marine Corps pacification program in the Marine Corps enclaves in I Corps. Because of the importance and the clarity of the pacification mission the CAPs were given when Corson took command, whether or not they were an effective counterinsurgency concept was easier to determine because the CAPs were put to a greater test of their capabilities. The CAP program was now given an opportunity to prove itself in one of the most important missions for the Marine Corps in the Vietnam War.

CAP Organizational Problems Before Becoming a Separate Command

Since the start of the CAPs there were administrative problems which were not resolved until the CAPs were officially brought together as a separate command. Usually each CAP was technically a part of the closest infantry battalion, and this caused some problems with administration because the Marines' pay, supplies, and mail came through their battalion. As was often the case, the battalion to which the Marines were assigned might move to another location, but the CAP of which the Marines were members remained where it was. In these circumstances the Marines could leave the CAP and return to their battalion for the battalion's move. This was not likely, though, and usually the Marines stayed with their CAP while they were officially transferred to another battalion close to the CAP's location. When the Marines were officially transferred to a different battalion their service records were sent to the new battalion and sets of orders for the transfer were required. Many of the infantry battalions were frequently moved to new locations , and it is easy to see the administrative chaos which could result from these procedures.[6] A Marine who served in a CAP near Phu Bai in 1966 said, "Whoever moved into Phu Bai, that's who we became attached to. My mailing address changed every sixty days or so. I was attached to 1st Battalion, 4th Marines; 2nd Battalion, 4th Marines; 3rd Battalion, 4th Marines; 1st Battalion, 9th Marines; and 2nd Battalion, 9th Marines, without ever leaving the compound."[7] These problems could be confusing, but other problems were dangerous for the CAPs.

Before the CAPs were brought together as a separate command there were also problems because the infantry battalions to which the Marines in the CAP were assigned were responsible for providing supplies and equipment for the CAPs. The infantry battalions usually had too few supplies and too little equipment for themselves, and this meant the CAPs were not often given much. Because of this the CAPs were frequently forced to obtain adequate levels of supplies and equipment for their units through barter, purchase, or even theft. Another problem was that some of the battalion's equipment could be taken from the CAP when the battalion moved.[8] In fairness, the battalion also needed the equipment, but in one situation a battalion moved and "The first the CAP knew about it was when the battalion in that area come to get its PRC-25 radio and .50-caliber machine gun." Because these were taken "The CAP had its firepower greatly diminished and was out of touch with everyone else for about a week."[9]

Another important problem was that the infantry battalions often had difficulties coordinating their operations with those of the CAPs that were attached to them. The infantry battalions were responsible for coordinating the patrolling of the CAPs and the troops in their own battalions, and this could be confusing at times. However, it was important to ensure patrols from the two units did not come into contact with each other and fire by mistake because they might think the other force was a guerrilla unit. Also, the infantry battalions were responsible for providing infantry reaction forces and artillery support for the CAPs. When the infantry battalion remained in one location this arrangement usually worked well, but problems could arise if the battalion was moving for some reason.[10] Regarding situations such as these Colonel Noble L. Beck, the Third Marine Division Operations Officer said, "Most often the infantry battalions were on the move from one area to another while the combined action units normally remained in the same location. It was not infrequent that the infantry command was called upon to come to the aid of a combined action unit with its 'tail in a crack' in a situation unknown to the infantry commander in advance, and often this found him in an awkward tactical posture for response."[11]

The confusion and the danger which arose from these command arrangements were lessened when the CAPs were made a separate command.

The command and supply structure in which the CAPs operated before they became a separate command also had a negative effect on the morale of the CAPs. The administrative problems resulting from Marines being transferred from one battalion to another when a battalion left an area probably meant the Marines' pay, mail, and supplies could sometimes be delayed. This might seem to be a minor problem for the Marines, but it could be a detriment to their morale, and they were already in a stressful situation in the CAPs. Not being able to depend on adequate supplies and equipment from the infantry battalions for the CAPs' military operations was a more serious problem, though. The small number of men in the CAPs and their isolated positions made them vulnerable to attacks as it was, and if they did not have adequate supplies and equipment, they became even more vulnerable. Even though in some instances CAPs were able to acquire the supplies, the equipment, and the weapons they needed through barter, purchase, and theft, they would have been better prepared to defend themselves and to perform their counterinsurgency missions if they were given a guaranteed source for supplies and equipment.

At times, needing to rely on the infantry battalions for infantry reaction forces and artillery support also created dangerous situations for the CAPs. Often the infantry units were away from their usual battalion area on assigned missions. In situations such as these the CAPs might not have an infantry reaction force readily available to help them fight a large NVA or NLF unit. This was a significant problem because the CAP concept could only succeed if reaction forces were prepared to quickly help them when they were threatened with overwhelming forces. If this were not the case the CAPs were too vulnerable, and the

CAP concept was not feasible. Artillery support for the CAPs was not as significant a problem because the artillery did not usually move with the infantry units when they went on their missions. However, artillery support for the CAPs was important for the same reason the infantry reaction forces were important, and if the CAPs were attacked by a large force, artillery fire was critical. There could also be occasions when the artillery was firing missions in support of battalion operations, and this might mean those artillery support missions were given priority over artillery fire support missions for the CAPs. These problems created because the Marines in the CAPs were formally a part of the infantry battalions lessened the ability of the CAPs to perform their counterinsurgency mission, and some of these problems were serious enough to result in a number of CAPs being overrun.

These problems were not so much the fault of the infantry battalions as they were the fault of the organizational arrangement which assigned the Marines in the CAPs to the infantry battalions and assigned some responsibilities for the CAPs to the battalions. The infantry battalions and the CAPs were given very different missions, and it would not be realistic to expect the infantry battalions to sacrifice their performance on their assigned missions to support the CAP units. The CAPs suffered because at times they may have lacked supplies, equipment, infantry reaction forces, and artillery support, but the infantry battalions also suffered because their responsibility to the CAPs took their own material resources and had the potential to distract them from focusing on the other missions assigned to the battalions. Assigning the CAPs to the infantry battalions was a poor organizational arrangement which probably arose out of necessity rather than design when the CAP program was started. When the CAPs were formed into a separate command it looked as if many of these problems could be eliminated.

Organizing a Separate Command

When Corson took command of the CAPs in February 1967, he brought together a staff of people to develop his ideas of how the CAP program should be formed as an independent unit. Officially the infantry battalions were still responsible for the administrative, supply, equipment, combat support, and operational control requirements of the CAPs. Now, though, Corson and his staff began to plan the necessary organizational structure, or Table of Organization and Equipment (TO&E) as it was designated, so it would be ready when the CAPs were formally made a separate command. One of the people who was a member of Corson's staff at this time described Corson and the staff members as being enthusiastic and committed as they worked to create a structure for the new unit. He said, "We were just forming up and working the plans out, and the organization charts; and how this thing was going to mesh, and where we were going to put these units, and how were we going to train those outfits; how were we going to resupply them...."[12] By June the TO&E was completed, but the CAP program was still not officially an independent command.

In June 1967 General Robert Cushman replaced Walt as commander of IIIMAF, and his deputy commander for IIIMAF was Nickerson, who along with Krulak and Walt had asked Corson to take command of the CAP program. Cushman made Nickerson responsible for the program, and, in turn, Nickerson gave Corson most of the responsibility for the new CAP command. Corson soon developed the required standard operating procedure (SOP) that detailed the goals, the missions, and the chain of command for the CAP program. During June Corson strengthened the organizational structure of the new CAP program by forming a Combined Action Group (CAG) headquarters at Danang, and four CAGs were eventually operating by the summer of 1968. The CAGs worked at the province level in I Corps, and each

CAG supervised a number of Combined Action Companies (CACOs) operating at the district level. In turn, the CACOs controlled the various CAPs working in the villages in their respective districts.[13] These actions gave the CAP program a clear organizational structure for the command of the CAPs down to the village level.

In practice the organizational structure worked to send orders from the CAG to the CACO and then to the individual CAP. The Popular Forces in the CAPs were officially supposed to take their orders from the village chief. Normally, though, they received their orders from the district chief who had more power. The CAGs were placed close to a province headquarters and they gave administrative support to the CACOs under their supervision. In addition, the CAGs worked with the unit commanders and the province chiefs to determine the tactical areas of coordination (TAOCs) in which the CACOs would operate. In turn, the CACO headquarters were placed at district headquarters where they were responsible for organizing medical evacuation, air and artillery support, and infantry reaction forces for the CAPs the CACOs supervised. Each CAP had its own TAOC which it controlled, and any other unit wanting to conduct operations within the CAP's area needed to request permission from the district commander and the CACO commanding the CAP in the area. This practice was intended to prevent friendly forces from firing on each other in the mistaken belief they were confronting a guerrilla force. The plan for the new CAP program was impressive, but at this time the CAPs were still officially dependent on the infantry battalions for administrative, supply, equipment, combat support, and operational control purposes.[14]

In July 1967 the III Marine Amphibious Force (IIIMAF) changed the support and control arrangement for the CAPs so that they were no longer under the control of the infantry battalions, and the CAP program became a separate command reporting directly to IIIMAF. In the revised chain of command, the CAPs were responsible to the CACOs, the CACOs were responsible to the CAGs, and the CAGs were directly responsible to the IIIMAF. As commander of the new CAP program Corson supervised the various elements of the CAP organization, and he reported directly to Nickerson who was the deputy commander of IIIMAF.[15] The CAP program was now a separate unit, but there were problems associated with this new independence.

One of the problems had to do with receiving adequate supplies. The staff of the new CAP program was now free to plan the tactics, the training, and the other matters necessary for the CAPs, but they had inadequate access to supplies to accomplish their plans. In their zeal they resorted to scrounging and ingenuity. One of the CAP staff members at this time said when the first Combined Action Group headquarters was started they only had one jeep he thought they had stolen, and they used it to go to Danang where "There was this junkyard. And we used to go in there and get tires, axles, pieces and parts of jeeps and rebuild. We had … a couple of good mechanics. We got a couple of good frames and we actually started building our own vehicles…." The efforts used to get their own vehicles was matched by the creativity this same CAP staff member said was used to get other supplies. He said, "I'd get a guy from the *Chicago Sun-Times* in, and I'd say, 'Hey, look: We need this kind of supply. And we [can] get it from Sears Roebuck. And can you help us?' And goddamn if Sears didn't come through and give us some supplies."[16] The creativity the staff members used to get the supplies they needed is commendable, but their need to do this is also disturbing.

The CAPs were chosen to perform the important mission of pacification in the rear areas of the Marine enclaves, and they needed adequate support to do this. Making the CAPs a separate command made it possible for Corson to tailor an organization suited for helping the individual CAPs do their pacification work in the villages. Also, making the CAPs a separate command allowed the new CAP command to focus all its efforts solely on finding ways to help the CAPs with their counterinsurgency tasks. These were positive developments for Corson's new unit, but they should have been given adequate supplies and equipment to accomplish their mission. Marine Corps generals as prominent as Krulak, Walt, and Nickerson chose the CAP program for the purpose of pacifying the enclaves, and they should have made sure the program was sufficiently supplied to do the job. When the staff of the new CAP program was forced to find outside sources for supplies and equipment it distracted them from accomplishing their primary mission.

Training and the Selection of CAP Warriors

When the CAG was formed at Danang in June 1967 a permanent CAP school was established to ensure Marines going to the villages were trained for their mission. Prior to this, some of the Marines who went to the CAPs were given training, but often Marines did not receive any formal training. In the first JAC units at Phu Bai, Ek conducted a course of training, but this was not always the case. Some Marines were not given any special training before they were assigned to CAP units, and one reason for this was the increased demand for more Marines in the CAPs when the program was greatly expanded between June and December of 1966.[17] One Marine said he and others in his unit were asked if any of them wanted to volunteer to live in a Vietnamese village. He said he and a few others went but "The words CAC and CAP were never spoken, but that's what it was, a CAP outfit.... We had to meet one of the Marines at a break in the wire on the perimeter.... He took us into the ville." After this the Marine squad leader in the CAP gave the new Marines the only training they received to prepare them for duty.[18] The CAP school was started to give the Marines standard training for their counterinsurgency mission.

The CAP school Corson established at Danang was intended to give a concentrated, intensive counterinsurgency training course to all the Marines going to the CAPs. The training period for each Marine at the school was usually two weeks, and Corson knew this was insufficient time to accomplish much training. Regarding this he said he "Realized that it was not possible to transform these Marines into linguists or cultural anthropologists overnight." However, he thought "It was possible to teach them some of the customs, some of the history, some of the culture of Vietnam. Maybe then they would approach the Vietnamese in the hamlets as human beings."[19]

The syllabus for the school reflected Corson's thinking with classes in Vietnamese culture, Vietnamese history, *co tuong*, and Vietnamese language; civic action; Vietnamese politics, and the organization and the history of the PFs. The students were also given classes on the weapons, the tactics, and the organization of the NLF. For most of the Marines, the combat and tactically oriented classes were refresher classes in small-unit tactics, patrolling, first aid, basic map reading and compass reading, basic infantry weapons, requesting artillery fire and air strikes, medical evacuation, and other military subjects. As part of their training for the CAPs the students and local PFs conducted patrols around the perimeter of the school area at night.[20]

The syllabus for the CAP school in 1967 shows that much of the military subject training was practical and appropriate to prepare the Marines for the CAPs, and the students were taught classes on military subjects for over thirty-nine hours during the two weeks. The Marines were coming from infantry units, and this has been criticized as too much time to devote to teaching Marine infantrymen basic military skills in such an accelerated course.[21]

Most of the men in the CAP school were enlisted men below the rank of NCOs, though, and in a typical infantry unit map reading was usually done by either officers or NCOs, and this was true for planning and leading patrols, and for conducting small-unit tactics. Specially trained Marines from artillery units were with the infantry to call in artillery support when it was needed, and specially trained Marines who were often pilots were with the infantry units to call in air support. In addition, if an enlisted Marine in an infantry unit did not know how to operate a radio, for instance, he was usually not far from an NCO who would show him how to do it, or who would do it himself. In the CAPs, though, some of the enlisted men would be leading patrols comprised of other Marines and PFs. In the dangerous environment of the villages, the men leading the patrols needed excellent patrolling skills. This was true for the other military skills taught in the CAP school, also. Any Marine in a CAP needed to be able to call for artillery support or an infantry reaction force if a patrol were under heavy attack. If a CAP compound were overrun, any Marines not wounded or killed also needed to know how to operate all the weapons in the compound, and to know how to operate a radio to call for a reaction force.

Quite a bit of time in the school was devoted to teaching military skills, but it was important for every Marine in the CAPs to know these skills. Security in the villages was the initial, most important task in the villages, and poor security could be catastrophic for the CAPs.

In two weeks of school there was not enough time to teach the Marines very much of what they would need to know in the CAPs, but there was a poor distribution of instruction time given to the non-military subjects in the syllabus. Civic action was a subject in the syllabus but there were only a few hours of instruction devoted to it. Altogether, in fact, there were fewer than eight hours of total instruction in the school program for Vietnamese culture and civic action.

The game of *co tuong* that Corson saw as a way to establish good relations with the Vietnamese people was taught for eight hours in the school program.[22] The use of this game worked well in Phong Bac, but eight hours of instruction in the CAP school may have been excessive. One Marine who went to the school later said, "They said it's a traditional game and everybody plays it ... and we learned it. I've been here a little over three months now and I have not yet sat down and played a game.... In fact, I'd venture to say I haven't even seen a game ... since I've been here."[23] While there were eight hours of instruction for *co tuong*, there were only six hours of Vietnamese language instruction in the two-week program.[24]

One Marine who thought the training was good was Barry Goodson, who served in an infantry unit for a number of months before he volunteered for the CAPs. Goodson said his experience in the CAP school changed the way he felt about the war and the Vietnamese people. While he was in the infantry Goodson said he participated in burning huts and destroying villages, but he was not proud of having done this. An officer who gave the new students an orientation speech told them one of their responsibilities would be to train the PFs in the CAP, and he also told them they would have "The responsibility of living with your Vietnamese counterparts and helping them improve their lives and the lives of all the villagers in whatever small way you can think of." After the wholesale destruction he saw during his service in the infantry Goodson was enthusiastic about the idea of helping the Vietnamese people. He thought, "It's about time. Up until now we only thought of the people as simple idiots, or animals we could slaughter without a second thought."

As he learned about Vietnamese culture and language during the first week of the school his thinking continued to change, and he said, "I was beginning to feel a strong devotion towards helping these people...." This marked change in Goodson's thinking and his changed attitude toward the Vietnamese people show the worth of the school for Goodson. He also thought highly of the combat-oriented training he received.[25]

Much of the second week of Goodson's training in CAP school was devoted to combat related training he considered rigorous and intense. He and the members of his class studied guerrilla strategy, explosives, and survival methods, and they also practiced hand-to-hand combat and learned to use a wide variety of weapons. Goodson's description of his CAP school training implies he thought it was a concentrated, practical preparation for his CAP duty.[26]

It is easy in retrospect to criticize the CAP school for what it did not teach the Marines going to the CAPs, but given the circumstances at the time the school gave the Marines good training. Some of the most important generals in the Marine Corps determined pacification in the villages in the rear areas of the enclaves was necessary for the success of the Marine Corps enclave strategy, and Corson was given the mission of forming a new unit to accomplish that mission. The pressure Corson felt must have been immense as he tried as quickly as he could to make the CAP program a functioning expression of his knowledge and his experience. Corson's thinking regarding this initial training for the Marines entering the CAP program was expressed to some degree when he said, "I'm giving a little light direction, because what I'm trying to establish in that period of time is given the ingenuity, the initiative of these young men, give them a little guidance … 'You're going to be all alone, sergeant or corporal. And I've taught you enough to be able to do it on your own.' It's a risk."[27]

The military subjects were stressed in the CAP school, and this was appropriate because the counterinsurgency mission of security was the primary mission of the CAPs, and without good security in the villages none of the other counterinsurgency tasks could be accomplished. The non-military training was less extensive, but there was enough of it to make the men aware of some of the cultural challenges they faced. It looks as if time was of the essence in this situation, and priority was put on giving the Marines some good training in a short period of time, and then getting them to the CAPs in the villages where they were needed. With a school to train the CAP Marines operating, Corson began a more careful process to select Marines for duty in the CAPs.

Corson knew the individual Marines serving in the CAPs were the most important component of the CAP program, and because of this he created a list of requirements for the selection of prospective CAP recruits. Previously when the infantry units were told to send men to the CAPs, they were given guidelines to follow in selecting those men. Essentially, the infantry commanders were told to send Marines who performed well in combat, and who did not have behavior problems. Often this did not work well because it was in the interest of the infantry units to keep their best men, and the infantry units often sent their unwanted men to the CAPs. The infantry units were now required to send a specific number of men to the CAPs, and to ensure the CAPs had the sort of recruits he wanted for the program Corson developed a set of criteria. Among these were that a CAP recruit needed to be a volunteer for the program, he needed to have served in a combat unit in Vietnam for at least four months, he needed a good recommendation from his commanding officer, he could not have any recorded disciplinary infractions, and he could not be xenophobic. Corson's standards for the CAP Marine recruits were high, and he worked to make sure they were met.

Corson used his specified criteria to initially find recruits for the CAP program, but he used other methods to make his final selections. One of his most important qualifications was that the men not be xenophobic. If one Marine in a CAP exhibited hatred or even dislike for the Vietnamese people this could cause an entire village to be alienated from the Marines in the CAP, and ruin any good relations the CAP had developed.[28] To prevent problems such as these and others, Corson developed a questionnaire. He said, "there were certain questions. And I looked the kid in the eye, and I'd ask him a couple of questions and I'd say, 'Get out of here,' or, 'Come here, young man.'"

Corson was serious about getting the sort of men he thought were appropriate for the program and he personally interviewed as many as he could. As he interviewed them Corson said he was looking for particular qualities he thought made people empathetic human beings. He wanted to eliminate men who felt superior to or disdainful toward the Vietnamese. In describing the negative characteristics he was looking for, he said "They do it with kinetic movements, with their hands, they do it with their voice, they do it with their face 'I know better than you.' And they show it. Part of it is swagger some of it is body movements, body chemistry." Corson thought his experience gave him the ability to do this. "And you see, I survived the environment and I knew what offended. If a kid is naturally offensive, I don't have time." If a Marine did not meet Corson's standards he was sent back to his unit. Even after the Marines entered training Corson continued to observe them, and if he thought a man did not have the qualities Corson wanted for the CAP Marines, he would have him dismissed from the program.[29]

Corson's obsession for finding the right men for the CAPs was matched by his obsession with making the CAP idea work as a counterinsurgency concept. His driving motivation, he said, was to overcome the challenge of finding an effective means of pacification in Vietnam. Corson gave careful attention to choosing the commanders for the CAGs because he said the prospective commanders needed to accept the idea that the squad leaders in the CAPs knew the situation better than the officers did. For this reason, the CAG commanders needed to know their jobs well before they could tell the squad leaders what their mission responsibilities were, and the officers could not simply say they knew better because of their rank. This was difficult for many officers to accept, but each village was a unique situation, and the officers needed to understand the situations in the villages before they could advise the CAP squad leaders. In keeping with this idea, one of the fundamental principles Corson used for the CAP program was to give the CAPs what they needed, and not have them bring their problems to higher authorities until the problems became critical. Corson said he used his ideas and experience to train the CAP Marines, and then gave them a chance to fail on their own. When the Marines made a mistake, the situation was reconstructed and a way to correct it was discussed. With this flexible trial and error method Corson said he and the CAP Marines tried to find answers for the problems the Marines encountered in each CAP. Because of his desire to improve their performance, Corson often went on patrols with the CAPs.[30]

The lessons derived from the Phong Bac experiment were not applied in a mechanical fashion, Corson said. His pacification methods worked well in Phong Bac because he was able to find a number of skilled men in his battalion, and because of the social and economic situations in that hamlet. Other villages and hamlets had different situations, and they needed to be dealt with individually. Also, the CAPs were squads, and it was difficult to find many skilled men in units that small. Corson made suggestions to the CAPs based on the lessons he learned from the Phong Bac experiment, and the CAPs decided what they wanted to do based on what they thought was needed, and the skill level of the men in the CAPs.[31]

In the summer of 1967, the CAP program was in an excellent position to show whether or not it was a good counterinsurgency concept in the Vietnam War according to the standards set for this study. The CAPs were now part of a separate unit focused on the counterinsurgency mission of pacification in Vietnamese villages in the rear areas of the Marine enclaves, and they were no longer hampered by their previous organizational ties to the infantry battalions. Three of the most prominent generals in the Marine Corps had encouraged and authorized the creation of the new CAP unit because they thought the pacification mission in the villages was so critical, and they were giving the program their support. Probably because of the importance of this mission, the man the generals chose to command the new unit was an officer considered to be one of the most experienced counterinsurgency experts in the Marine Corps. In his capacity as the director of the new CAP program, Corson's knowledge of counterinsurgency warfare promised to help the CAPs develop their counterinsurgency abilities. A formal school was also established to give the Marines going to the CAPs a course of training for the specialized work they would be doing in the villages. For the most part the training the Marines were given in the school was practical and adequate for the work they were expected to do, and it was assumed they would learn more of what they needed to know from the other men in the CAPs to which they were assigned. With the CAPs a separate unit focused on counterinsurgency, and a school to train the CAP Marines operating, Corson began to put his plan into practice.

Chapter 7

CAP Performance as a Counterinsurgency Concept

The Combined Action Platoon Command was at a pivotal moment in its history at this time, and as Corson carefully shaped the CAP program, he gave the CAPs a list of six specific missions to accomplish. These missions were the same missions the PF units were previously given during the war, for the most part, but by themselves the PFs had difficulties completing them. Corson was confident the Marines and the PFs together could successfully perform the missions. "And for the first time since we have confronted a war of national liberation, we know how to defeat the Communists in an insurgency environment."[1]

The missions Corson gave the CAPs dealt with most of the missions this study determined the CAPs needed to accomplish to be considered a successful counterinsurgency concept in the Vietnam War. In the opinion of this study the most basic responsibility of the CAPs was to provide security for the Vietnamese people by keeping the guerrillas away from the villages. This security effort of the CAPs also needed to block the guerrillas from having access to the villages to obtain the food, recruits, supplies, and intelligence they needed. The CAPs also needed to find and eliminate the NLF agents or members of the guerrilla infrastructure among the people in the village. The CAP members had to gain the loyalty of the people and develop intelligence sources. The CAPs also needed to perform civic action and economic development projects to improve the living standards and the economic conditions of the villages. Psychological operations needed to be conducted to discredit the NLF and to promote the loyalty of the villagers to the central government. Finally, the local government had to be developed and strengthened to help improve the control of the central government over the villages.

The six missions Corson gave the CAPs were:

1. Destroy the NLF within the village hamlet area of responsibility.
2. Protect public security and help maintain law and order.
3. Protect the friendly infrastructure.
4. Protect bases and lines of communication within the villages and hamlets.
5. Organize people's intelligence nets [*sic:* networks].
6. Participate in civic action and conduct propaganda against the NLF.[2]

Later Corson described how he thought the CAPs accomplished these six counterinsurgency missions during the time he commanded the CAP program. He said the CAPs worked to destroy the NLF in the village hamlet area of responsibility in three ways that complemented each other. The military security in the CAP villages was excellent, and this prevented guerrillas from entering the villages to recruit fighters for the NLF. As proof of this, extensive CAP census-taking operations found that few people left the areas the CAPs controlled, and Corson said this indicated not many people left the areas to join the NLF. In a similar way, the NLF could not take rice from the villagers because the CAPs guarded the village rice harvests. The local markets were also watched to ensure people were not purchasing large amounts of rice or other supplies which might be smuggled to the NLF. Corson said these methods were effective because some NLF prisoners and defectors stated the guerrillas thought it was dangerous to attempt to get rice and supplies from villages where there were CAPs, and because of this they chose to go to villages where there were no CAPs. In these ways the first two measures denied the guerrillas the recruits, the rice, and the supplies they needed to exist as a guerrilla movement.

The third way the CAPs worked to destroy the NLF was through the combat operations the CAPs conducted in the areas of the villages. Here the CAPs fought the guerrillas and showed their ability and willingness to defend the villages from the NLF forces. So, Corson said the CAP security operations accomplished the mission of destroying the NLF by killing its fighters, and by preventing the NLF from getting the recruits, the supplies, and the intelligence needed to sustain the NLF insurgency.[3]

The security to eliminate guerrilla activity in and around the villages also helped the CAPs accomplish the second, third, and fourth missions Corson gave the CAPs. The continual series of patrols and ambushes the CAPs conducted prevented the NLF from interfering with the business and social activities in the villages. The NLF tax collectors, recruiters, and propaganda teams were kept out of the villages by the CAPs so the people could live, farm, and do business in an atmosphere of relative peace and stability. Often the CAPs served as both the security force and the police force for the villages, and in some situations, they helped resolve differences between people in the villages.

As proof the CAPs were able to protect the leadership and the infrastructures of the villages, Corson said his research showed in villages without CAPs only 29 percent of the hamlet chiefs felt safe enough to stay in their homes during the night. In contrast, in villages where there were CAPs over 80 percent of the hamlet chiefs felt safe enough to stay in the villages throughout the day and the night. Also, there were operating hamlet councils in 93 percent of the villages where CAPs were located, while only twenty-nine percent of the hamlets in villages without CAPs had operating hamlet councils.[4]

Good security operations and the establishment of good relations with the Vietnamese people helped the CAPs accomplish their fifth mission of creating effective intelligence operations in the villages, Corson said. He stressed the importance good intelligence plays in defeating an insurgency, and he said the first requirement for getting intelligence from the people is the existence of good security measures in the villages. Rather than staying in the villages for a period of time and then leaving, as other Marine and ARVN units had, the CAPs lived among the people and protected them from the NLF. Some of the people came to trust the CAPs because they stayed in the villages, and they also saw the CAPs were able to fight and defeat the guerrillas. The Marines simply treated the people in a humane manner, and they did not attempt an ideological crusade against the communists. Interestingly, Corson said the affection the young Marines showed for the children frequently led to friendships which resulted in the children being the first villagers to bring intelligence information to the CAPs.

Eventually some of the other villagers saw that the Marines and the PFs in the CAPs protected the people and treated them well, and they began to provide more intelligence about guerrilla activities. Corson thought this process of treating the people humanely and proving they could defend the people from the NLF was an excellent way for the CAPs to gain intelligence. In fact, the intelligence program began to work so well that after six months in operation many CAPs were receiving more intelligence information than they were able to act upon with their own resources.[5]

The civic action portion of the sixth CAP mission was initiated after some progress toward achieving the first five missions was accomplished. This was done partly because civic action worked best when the CAPs attained the confidence and the goodwill of at least some of the people, and performing the first five CAP missions helped them to do this. Establishing military security was the paramount mission for the CAPs in the villages, and all of the CAP resources were focused on accomplishing this before any appreciable amount of time and resources could be used for civic action or any of their other missions. Also, the Marines wanted to find out what civic action projects the people themselves wanted in the village instead of trying to tell them what they needed. As the Marines lived in the villages and worked to perform their first five missions, they developed a rapport with the people and the people eventually felt confident in telling the Marines what civic action projects they wanted.[6]

After the Marines gained the confidence of the villagers there were few limitations to the civic action projects the Marines could help complete in the villages, Corson thought. The Marines used their initiative and imagination to think of potential civic action projects they could suggest to the people, and among the successful projects were road and bridge repairs, new farming techniques, field irrigation, credit unions, and school construction. The Marines learned the projects would fail if they became impatient and did all the work themselves. The villagers needed to maintain their self-respect by knowing the projects were primarily the result of their own work, and the Marines could help, but they needed to allow the people to work at their own pace.[7]

Corson thought the Marines accomplished their final mission of propaganda through their actions. By simply acting in a humane manner toward the Vietnamese people the Marines disproved many of the negative NLF accusations regarding the Americans. The Marines and the PFs also caused some defections from the NLF with the propaganda technique of personally encouraging villagers with relatives among the guerrillas to tell those relatives to quit the NLF. The CAP members did this patiently and without using pressure, but they explained the relatives among the guerrillas would eventually be found and possibly killed if they stayed with the NLF. By staying in the villages the CAPs countered one of the strongest NLF propaganda messages. The NLF guerrillas always said they would fight their way back into the villages, but the NLF was never able to reoccupy any village where a CAP was established.[8]

The missions the CAPs conducted in the villages were important, and there were three reasons for the success of the CAPs, in Corson's thinking. First, the squad of Marines and the Navy corpsman in the CAP were never more than fifteen men, and a force this small did not threaten to upset the traditional social network within the village. This small group of Marines and a corpsman also tried to be respectful and friendly, and they worked to adjust to the social norms of the villages. The second reason for success was the ability of the Marines to prove they and the PFs in the CAPs were a strong enough military force to protect the villages. The third reason was that the youth and the rank of the enlisted Marines in the CAPs made it easier for the PFs and people in the villages to identify with the Marines as people similar to themselves.[9]

The most significant reason for the success of the CAPs, in Corson's opinion, was the idealism the Marines exhibited for their mission in the CAPs. The people knew most of the Marines in the CAPs volunteered for the dangerous duty, and through their actions the Marines demonstrated their commitment to their stated mission to help the people. The people had frequently heard empty promises from Americans and GVN representatives who came to the villages and then left after a short period of time. In contrast, the CAP Marines lived and sometimes died among the people as they helped the PFs fight the guerrillas. As they shared the dangers with the people the young Marines also tried to help the Vietnamese improve the living conditions in their villages, and they made a sincere effort to respect the culture of Vietnam.[10]

Corson's evaluation of the CAP program probably involved some bias on his part. He created and directed the program as a separate command. Still, because of Corson's counterinsurgency expertise his evaluation of the performance of the CAPs is valuable in determining whether or not the CAP program was an effective counterinsurgency concept during the Vietnam War. His analysis shows the CAPs were doing an excellent job in most respects, but he did not specifically address some areas. The greatest strength of the CAPs was their ability to secure the villages from the NLF. As Corson said, the NLF never regained control of a village where a CAP was stationed. Even in those instances when a CAP unit was overrun, other Marines were quickly brought to the villages and the CAPs continued to operate. CAP security measures made it difficult for the NLF to recruit soldiers, and census operations conducted by the CAPs showed few people left the villages in which CAPs were located. Because of tight security, NLF prisoners and defectors said the guerrillas were forced to attempt to obtain rice and other supplies from villages where there were no CAPs. Corson did not directly address how the CAP security attempted to keep villagers from giving intelligence information to the NLF, but it can be assumed sending intelligence to the NLF was more difficult because of the constant watchfulness of the CAP members and their sympathizers. Corson's evaluation supports the conclusion that the CAPs were performing almost all of their counterinsurgency security tasks well.

In his analysis of the CAPs performance Corson did not discuss specifically how any hidden members of the NLF infrastructure were eliminated. Again, though, it can be assumed the activities of the hidden agents were inhibited or ended by the security activities of the CAPs, and some of the individual agents were detected through the intelligence activities of the CAPs. One of the most important functions of the hidden NLF agents in the villages was to supply the guerrillas with recruits, rice, other supplies, and intelligence. Because of the extensive security measures of the CAPs, if the agents attempted to send supplies to the guerrillas they would probably have been caught. As the intelligence network of the CAPs became more extensive, the hidden NLF agents faced a greater chance of being discovered by the CAPs, and this could cause the agents to be less active. It is likely that both the security measures and the intelligence networks of the CAPs either discovered the agents or caused them to be inactive, for the most part.

Assuming the security and the intelligence actions of the CAPs eliminated the hidden agents or hindered their activities is not adequate, though. Considering Corson's background in intelligence and the threat posed by the hidden NLF infrastructure in the villages, it is surprising he did not specifically address how this threat could be eliminated. Even though the actions of the hidden agents may have been hampered by the operations of the CAPs, the agents were still capable of harming the CAPs and intimidating the villagers. It is probable the agents could find some way to send messages to the guerrillas, and they could give the guerrillas information regarding the strength, the defenses, and the daily routines of the CAP members. These agents could also tell the guerrillas which villagers were helping the CAPs, and the agents could also carry out assassinations on their own. These were some of the reasons the hidden agents were a formidable problem for the counterinsurgency efforts in the villages, and the CAPs needed to find a way to eliminate them.

The local government of the CAP villages were strengthened, but Corson did not say this was done to help improve the control of the GVN over the villages. Part of the reason Krulak, Walt, and Nickerson chose to bring the CAPs together as a separate command was their belief the GVN and the ARVN could not adequately perform the pacification themselves. The generals thought this because previous pacification efforts showed the GVN and the ARVN were inept, unwilling, and corrupt. A lesson for future pacification projects Corson drew from the Phong Bac experiment was that the Marines performing pacification missions needed to actively confront anyone from either the NLF or the GVN who tried to corrupt or destroy their program.

In his evaluation of the performance of the CAPs, Corson said good security in the CAP villages made it possible for the majority of the hamlet chiefs to remain in their villages without the threat of being killed by the guerrillas. Because good security kept the NLF from interfering with them, the majority of villages where there were CAPs also had functioning hamlet councils. Corson's evaluation of the CAP program shows the counterinsurgency task of developing and strengthening the local government was accomplished by the CAPs, but there was little if any effort to improve the control of the GVN over the villages.

Problems for the CAP Program

Corson's evaluation showed the CAPs were doing well in accomplishing their assigned missions in the villages, but there were exceptions among the CAPs. It must have been difficult to attempt to maintain high standards for the large number of CAPs scattered across a large geographical area. Major Max McQuown commanded a Marine infantry battalion with two CAPs located in two villages within the battalion's TAOR, and he was not impressed with the CAPs. He said, "Few of the Marines assigned to these two CAP units had prior ground combat experience.... The leaders and the Marines under them ... lacked skills in scouting and patrolling, mines and booby traps, map reading, observed fire procedures, basic infantry tactics, and VC tactics and techniques." In addition to criticizing the military knowledge of the CAP Marines, McQuown also said, "They had scant knowledge of the Vietnamese language and were unfamiliar with the social and religious customs of the people they were living with." His criticism included the relations the Marines and the PFs had with the villagers, and he said the Marine and the PF "Members of the CAP platoon kept themselves aloof from the villagers they were supposed to be helping...." The village chiefs thought the two CAPs were so ineffective that "Neither chief had faith that the CAP would accomplish anything."[11] The CAPs may have been doing well in most respects in 1967, but this statement shows some of them still had problems.

Earlier in the war both Walt and Krulak decided the Marines in Vietnam needed to understand that an important part of their mission was the protection of the Vietnamese people, and in an effort to find ways to help eliminate any negative feelings the Marines had for the Vietnamese people, Krulak authorized a program called the Personal Response Project. The person chosen to lead the new program was Richard McGonigal, who was a trained sociologist as well as a US Navy chaplain, and McGonigal began to conduct a series of attitudinal surveys in the various Marine units. Although McGonigal began his work before Corson assumed command of the CAPs, eventually he and Corson met, and soon McGonigal was helping Corson with the CAP program.[12]

It looks as if McGonigal thought the CAP program Corson was planning could perform its pacification mission well, and he began to work closely with Corson. He helped Corson write the questionnaire Corson used to interview prospective CAP Marines, and in some instances, he helped with the interviews. When the CAP school began, McGonigal also played a significant role in forming its curriculum. Among the classes he developed for the new school were classes in Vietnamese language, customs, and history. As McGonigal worked with the program he continued to conduct attitudinal surveys among the CAP Marines.[13]

A Personal Response Project survey report on the attitudes of Marines in I Corps toward South Vietnamese military and civilians was completed in 1967, and it revealed some disturbing information about those attitudes. Twenty-two percent of the Marines in the CAPs said they disliked the Vietnamese military, and 17 percent said they had mixed feelings toward the Vietnamese military. As far as Vietnamese civilians were concerned, 10 percent of the CAP Marines said they disliked the civilians, and 20 percent said they had mixed feelings toward the civilians.[14]

These figures must have caused some concern among the officers in charge of the CAP program. The survey was initiated in October 1966, and this was well before Corson took command of the CAP program in February 1967, but the survey continued through June 1967. The results of the survey showed 39 percent of the Marines in the CAPs either did not like the Vietnamese PFs with whom they served, or they disliked them to some degree. Also, 30 percent of the CAP Marines either disliked the villagers or they disliked them to some extent. Because the Marines in the CAPs worked so closely with the PFs and the Vietnamese civilians, these attitudes would be difficult to hide. This means that roughly one-third of the Marines in the CAPs did not like the PFs and the civilians, or they did not like them very much.

Corson's analysis showed the CAP program was performing well by the end of 1967, but the comments of some of the

CAP Marines and the results of the survey show there were still important problems to be addressed. The CAP program became a separate unit under Corson's command in February 1967, though, and it is not realistic to imagine Corson could have made it into the instrument of pacification he wanted it to be in a few short months. Many of the Marines serving in the CAPs were in the program before Corson began his careful selection screening process, and the CAP school which gave a uniformity of training to the Marines was not established until June 1967.

In discussing his relationships with the Marines and the PFs in his CAP platoon, one Marine made an important point related to the results of McGonigal's survey. He said his relations with the members of the CAP platoon were the same as they were in any other group of people; he had some close friends, he liked others, and he did not like some of the people.[15] These might simply have been problems associated with the initial growth of a new organization, and if it were given time, the program Corson had in place showed the promise of being able to eliminate many, although probably not all, of these problems.

The CAPs at the End of 1967

A major change occurred in the new CAP program when Corson completed his tour of duty in South Vietnam in August 1967 and returned to the United States. Corson must have thought he left the program in good hands when he chose a specialist in counterinsurgency named Lieutenant Colonel Russ Hittenger, as his successor. However, Hittenger was killed before he assumed command, and Lieutenant Colonel Brunnenmeyr took command of the program. Brunnenmeyr only commanded the CAP program for three months before he was replaced by a Marine infantry officer named Lieutenant Colonel Byron F. Brady.[16]

By the end of 1967 the CAPs looked as if they might be able to succeed at the necessary counterinsurgency tasks they were assigned. As a separate command, the CAP program mission statement focused on the performance of many of those tasks, and the training for the Marines was calculated to help them accomplish those counterinsurgency tasks in the villages. There were problems, but they did not look as if they were problems which could not be solved with good organization, good training, and good leadership.

However, the pacification program in which the CAPs played a central role was no longer the primary concern of the Marine Corps by the end of 1967. During the year the Marine Corps sent more of its troops to the area of South Vietnam below the Demilitarized Zone (DMZ) to counter an increasing number of NVA units operating there. The threat of an invasion of South Vietnam by the NVA appeared greater toward the end of the year as they laid siege to the Marine base at Khe Sanh, and there was concern they might try to overrun the base. Marine infantry units combed through the jungles and the hills below the DMZ, and they fought fierce battles with NVA forces supported by artillery fired from dug-in positions in North Vietnam and the DMZ. In addition to the base at Khe Sanh, Marines were also needed to defend other static positions such as Con Thien and Camp Carroll. Many of the resources and much of the attention of the Marine Corps were devoted to this semi-conventional war being fought along the DMZ, and this could only mean fewer resources and less attention was given to the pacification program of which the CAPs were a central part.

Chapter 8

TET and a Changing Role for the Combined Action Platoons

During 1967 some developments promised to help the Combined Action Platoons realize any potential they had as a counterinsurgency concept. There were events beyond the control of the program during 1967, though, which hampered their progress.

The increased level of fighting in the area of the Demilitarized Zone (DMZ) during 1967 was one of the central reasons the CAP program was hindered in developing as well as it might have. Fighting along the DMZ intensified as the Marines fought hard battles with an increasing number of North Vietnamese Army regular units infiltrating into South Vietnam. The Marine infantry battalions needed every man they had for these fights, and their casualty rates were high during this time. As a result of this they were not in a position to send many, if any, men to the CAPs. A great deal of Marine Corps air and artillery support was also needed for the fighting near the DMZ, and this meant there was a decrease in the amount of air and artillery support available for the CAPs. At the start of 1967 there were fifty-seven CAPs operating and the intention was to have 114 by the end of the year. Partly because of the manpower needs of the infantry units only seventy-nine CAPs were operating by the end of 1967.[1]

Because of the problems the program had in finding an adequate number of Marines, the program changed its requirements for prospective CAP Marines during 1967. Corson initially said all the CAP recruits needed to have served a minimum of four months in a combat unit before they came to the CAPs, but this stipulation was dropped. Also, Corson's requirement that none of the CAP recruits have any recorded disciplinary actions was no longer in effect. However, the standards for new recruits were still high. These were the formalized standards for CAP recruits in 1967:

1. Have been in-country for at least two months if on first tour or have served a previous tour.
2. Have a minimum of six months remaining on current tour or agree to extend to meet this requirement.
3. Be a volunteer and motivated to live and work with the Vietnamese people.
4. Be a mature, motivated Marine and recommended by his commanding officer.
5. Had no nonjudicial punishment within the past three months, not more than one nonjudicial punishment and no courts-martial within the past year.
6. Have an average 4.0 marks in conduct and proficiency with last marks at least 4.0.
7. Have not received more than one Purple Heart award on current tour.
8. Preferably a high school graduate.[2]

These standards were high enough to ensure the CAPs had good candidates for the program, and experience may have shown the previous standards were unnecessarily high. By this time all CAP recruits went through the CAP school, and the school gave them good, realistic training for their duty. Also, their best training was given to them by the more experienced CAP members when they arrived at their new CAP assignments.

When Corson left Vietnam and command of the CAP program in August 1967 it may have had a negative effect on the ability of the CAPs to show how well they could work as a counterinsurgency concept. When he organized the CAP program Corson used his counterinsurgency expertise and his experience from the Phong Bac experiment to form the program's structure to accomplish the pacification mission. He also personally chose the officers he wanted as his subordinates, and in many instances, he personally chose the individual Marines. The new CAP program was Corson's creation, and he was an integral part of it.

In addition to his experience, Corson also brought his own charisma to the program, and this translated into a sense of spirit and vision which appears to have given a sense of purpose and confidence to the CAP Marines. One CAP veteran said Corson "Saw the Program's potential and expanded it into a formalized and integrated instrument of true pacification." He continued to say Corson also "Gave the Program a unique style…."[3] When another CAP veteran discussed Corson he said, "Nobody except a few really understood what our job was." He said, though "Col. Bill Corson, the first director, was very instrumental in the program and always supported us—he knew what we were about."[4] After he organized the CAP program and commanded it for approximately six months, Corson left Vietnam to return to the United States.

It is difficult to understand why Corson left when he did. Corson was chosen for the high-priority mission of pacifying the Vietnamese villages, and he was given the CAPs to form as an independent command to accomplish the job.

This was a unique assignment that capitalized on Corson's talents and experience, but he never offered an adequate explanation for leaving after six months.

Corson began writing his book, *The Betrayal*, soon after he left Vietnam, and the book was published in 1968 after Corson had retired from the Marine Corps. In his book Corson detailed his disgust with the way the war was being fought, but he said the war could still be won if it were fought in a different manner. Corson believed strongly in the CAPs as a counterinsurgency concept, and he saw them as a key part in a changed military strategy. A point in the strategy he proposed in his book was "Merging and placing the Regional and Popular Forces under direct US command to form a massive Combined Action Program." Included in this program would be "A US contribution of approximately 60,000 troops. This force would be used to provide relevant and credible military security in 3,500 to 3,750 … hamlets."[5] While Corson thought highly of the CAP program, it looks as if he thought he could do more to change what he saw as a misdirected war by having his book published than by leading the CAP program.

TET

Toward the end of 1967 intelligence information began to indicate that the NVA and the NLF were preparing for a major offensive in South Vietnam. In the I Corps area, captured NVA prisoners said they were told to prepare for a conclusive battle, and intelligence determined NVA units in the DMZ area were being reinforced. Intelligence sources also confirmed additional NVA divisions were moving into positions close to the Marine base at Khe Sanh. As a result of this information William Westmoreland considered what his response should be.[6]

Westmoreland reviewed this intelligence and intelligence from various other sources and concluded the NLF and the NVA were probably going to conduct a large offensive somewhere in South Vietnam, and he began to consider where the offensive might occur. In December 1967 Westmoreland sent a message to Washington saying he thought the NLF and the NVA would try to achieve a significant victory to give them a position of strength before they agreed to negotiations. In his opinion, Westmoreland thought the NVA would attack and attempt to overwhelm the Marine base at Khe Sanh. As a result of this, Westmoreland ordered the Marine Corps to send additional forces to the camp, and to increase the number of Marine units operating in the area around the base.[7]

Krulak's thinking regarding the matter differed from Westmoreland's. Krulak had been opposed to the plan when Westmoreland decided to establish a Marine base at Khe Sanh in 1966, and he thought Westmoreland only intended to use the camp to lure the NVA into a siege in which their forces could be destroyed by US air power. Krulak looked at the NVA activity in the DMZ area and around Khe Sanh and sent a cable to Walt saying he thought the NVA was attempting to draw the Marines away from the successful pacification work the Marines were performing in I Corps. From the perspective of the NVA, Krulak thought the pacification the Marine Corps was accomplishing was seen by the NVA "As the greatest threat to my aspirations on the Indochina Peninsula." In order to remove the threat, the NVA was "Applying Mao's tactical doctrine, 'Uproar in the East, Strike in the West.'" Krulak saw the increased NVA willingness to send its forces into the DMZ area to fight the Marines as a diversion. He thought the NVA was glad to have its forces fight the Marines in the DMZ area because the Marines "Might otherwise be engaged in Revolutionary Development Support [the official term for pacification]...." Krulak concluded his prescient cable to Walt by saying "We may expect him [the enemy] to hang on to our forces in Quang Tri as long as he can."[8]

On the night of January 30 and the morning of January 31, 1968, the Tet offensive struck throughout South Vietnam with surprise and fury. Taking advantage of a ceasefire declared to celebrate Tet, the Vietnamese Lunar New Year, the NLF and the NVA assaults included attacks on five of the six principal cities and thirty-six of South Vietnam's forty-four provincial capitals.[9] The effect of the attacks on Saigon were negated to some extent because US Army Lieutenant General Fred Weyand had earlier evaluated intelligence reports as indicating there were large NLF and NVA forces moving into the area close to Saigon. Because of these reports some forces were put on alert, and Weyand had US forces in position to defend Saigon when the Tet attacks began.

Ironically, the ineffectiveness of the search and destroy tactics was demonstrated when one of the most significant attacks on Saigon came from the historically NLF-dominated region called the Iron Triangle. The attack came from this area even though in 1967 various large-scale search and destroy operations, including the massive Operation Cedar Falls, were conducted there.[10] At Khe Sanh the attack was not as intense as Westmoreland expected.

A series of attacks by the NVA on the base at Khe Sanh had begun on January 20, 1968, but they were an effort to divert attention and resources from the general attacks initiated at the end of the month. A former NVA colonel later said, "A few weeks before Tet, a diversion was created with the attack launched against Khe Sanh. The Khe Sanh maneuver was intended to lull the cities and municipalities into a false sense of security."[11] The NVA commanders in the DMZ area were given instructions to draw in and engage as many US and ARVN forces as they could. At Khe Sanh the NVA staged two infantry attacks within three days, but neither was made by a force larger than a regiment. Unfortunately for the Marines, a well-placed NVA artillery bombardment exploded Khe Sanh's central ammunition dump, and this created severe problems for the camp's defenders. In response to these events Westmoreland ordered a massive bombing campaign around Khe Sanh, and two additional infantry battalions were sent to help in the defense of the camp. Westmoreland prepared Khe Sanh for the main attack he expected, but instead the main attack exploded as a series of coordinated attacks throughout South Vietnam.[12]

One of the most important counterinsurgency tasks for the CAPs was to gather intelligence, and prior to the Tet offensive their intelligence gave indications attacks were coming. Byron Brady was the program director during this period, and he credited the CAPs with providing the first and the best intelligence reports, which caused the IIIMAF to cancel the Tet ceasefire agreement with the NLF before the attacks started.[13]

Before the Tet attacks began, a number of CAPs were reporting an increase in NLF and NVA activity in the areas of their villages, and they also reported information signaling an attack might take place. One CAP Marine said, "For a week or more our village had suddenly been filled with strange young men in civilian clothes." In another village a Marine said, "Early in December 1967 some of the villagers started asking me to give them sandbags…. I changed the [patrol] routine by going into some of the houses…. The villagers were actually digging in." While they were on a daytime patrol on January 12, 1968, members of this same CAP were ambushed by a force they later discovered was part of an NVA regiment which had only recently arrived in the area.[14] Because they lived and worked in and around the Vietnamese villages the CAP members were uniquely able to discover and submit intelligence information such as this.

Although Brady said he was grateful for the intelligence he received from the CAPs, some Marines thought intelligence they submitted prior to the Tet offensive was disregarded. On one occasion a patrol found a map made in the ground marked with all the CAP village locations in the area. The information was passed on through intelligence channels, but no action was taken, and the people to whom the Marines sent the information said, "They got that stuff all the time." A member of the CAP which discovered the map later said, "That was one of the problems with the CAPs—we didn't have any officers with us. They thought we exaggerated." Some Marines became frustrated when CAP intelligence on NLF and NVA troop movements was disregarded because "We were not listened to by higher command…. We watched heavy weapons squads come in, platoons come in, and we called these. And nobody believed us…." Less credence may have been given to the intelligence reports of the CAPs because there were no officers with them and in this instance the Marines said they "Were told by higher ups that, quote, we didn't know what the hell we were talking about…. Nobody would bother to check it out."[15] Even though some of the information they provided was not given much serious attention, the CAPs showed they were capable of gathering important intelligence prior to the Tet attacks.

Many of the CAPs were attacked during the Tet offensive, and the attacks usually came when the NLF and the NVA forces were either on their way to assault one of the cities or when they were returning from one of those attacks. Some CAP Marines thought the program was considered such a threat that one of the objectives of the NLF and the NVA units was to destroy the CAPs. The number of attacks on the CAPs during the Tet offensive gives some support to this possibility. From January through October 1967, approximately 14 percent of the NLF and NVA attacks in the I Corps area were made on CAPs. From November preceding the Tet offensive through the middle of January 1968, 47 percent of the attacks in the I Corps area were directed at CAPs. Also, the number of contacts with NLF and

NVA forces from December 1967 through most of January 1968 averaged approximately five per week for each CAP. These numbers increased dramatically to an average of approximately fifteen contacts each week from January twenty-ninth through February ninth. During the period of the Tet offensive, sixty-nine of the CAPS stayed in their villages, and nine were either temporarily moved to another location to provide security, or they were temporarily moved after they were overrun by NLF and NVA forces.[16]

In one instance during the Tet offensive, two CAP platoons were especially important in the defense of the city of Danang. The two CAPs were positioned directly in the path NVA troops were using in their approach to attack Danang, and two NVA divisions assaulted them with overwhelming force. When Corson later described the fight of the two CAPs during the NVA attack, he compared it to the suicidal Spartan defense at Thermopylae during the Persian Wars. Although they were massively outnumbered, the CAPs stood and fought to protect their villages. There was no possibility the Marines and the PFs could survive an assault by a force that large, but they fought as long as they could. In the end approximately twenty-seven Marines and an undetermined number of PFs were killed; one Marine survived the battle when he was left for dead by the attacking NVA. The defense provided by the CAPs slowed the advance of the NVA, though, and the time gained by their defensive efforts allowed Marine infantry units to be brought into the fight to attack and defeat the NVA divisions. One result of this battle was that the city of Danang was the only major city in South Vietnam the NLF and the NVA did not attack during the Tet offensive.[17]

In the drastic circumstances of the Tet offensive, the CAPs usually did well in accomplishing their primary counterinsurgency task of protecting their villages. The attacks of the NLF and the NVA were almost exclusively directed at the cities of

South Vietnam, but when the NLF and the NVA forces passed by CAP villages they often attacked them. In a few instances the CAPs were ordered to leave their villages for purposes such as providing security at strategic bridge locations and along important highways. When this happened the CAP members did it reluctantly, and they were adamant that they wanted to stay and protect their villages. A number of CAPs were attacked and virtually annihilated during the Tet offensive, as they sometimes were on other occasions, but the Marines killed were always quickly replaced. In the NVA assault on the two CAPs defending the route to Danang only one of the Marines survived, but the next day Marines were sent to those villages to serve in the CAPs. This was done to show the people the Marines might be killed, but the CAPs would not be abandoned.[18]

The extent, the surprise, and the coordination of the Tet offensive shocked Westmoreland and some members of the US government in Washington. On the morning of January 31, 1968, Westmoreland went to the US embassy in Saigon where a group of NLF commandos had fought their way onto the embassy grounds during the previous night. In a hard fight the last of the commandos were finally either killed or captured, and Westmoreland now stood in the ruins of the embassy and gave an informal press conference. His comments to the press could be construed as indicating he was completely bewildered by the situation he faced as a result of the NLF and the NVA attacks throughout South Vietnam. He said the attacks were "very deceitfully" conceived to create concern in South Vietnam, and he stated the primary NVA attack would still come at Khe Sanh.[19]

The MACV commander's lack of comprehension of the situation was possibly exceeded by how stunned President Johnson and some others in Washington appeared to be when they received news of the Tet offensive. Lyndon Johnson's White House secretary at the time was George Christian, and he said,

"The Tet offensive came as a brutal surprise to President Johnson and all of his advisors." He said the reason for this was that "We had been led to believe that the Viet Cong were pretty well defanged by that period, that the pacification program had worked very well, that most of the villages in South Vietnam were secure, and that it was virtually impossible for the Viet Cong to rise to the heights that they did in 1968."[20] At a minimum, the strategy and the tactics used to fight the war were now called into question.

The historian Lewis Sorley later gave a depressing summary of the results of almost three years of the US war in South Vietnam in the aftermath of the Tet offensive. He said Westmoreland's strategy of attrition killed large numbers of NLF and NVA fighters, but these were losses the NLF and the NVA were willing to take, and they were replaced without much difficulty. As US troops conducted the search and destroy operations in the remote jungles and mountains of the country, the NLF was able to maintain and extend its control over the Vietnamese people in the rural areas without significant interference. Even though the NLF and the NVA were suffering many casualties, they appeared willing to accept these losses because they were peripheral to their ability to accomplish their primary objective. The NLF and the NVA understood gaining the allegiance of the people would win this insurgency war for them, and they were focused on that objective.[21] Previously the strategy of attrition seemed foolish; now it appeared increasingly criminal.

The fighting during Tet was brutal and obscene, and during this time many Vietnamese civilians either became more confirmed in their beliefs, or the uncommitted finally gave their allegiance to one side or the other. In his book, *A Vietcong Memoir*, Truong Nhu Tang said some South Vietnamese intellectuals committed themselves to the NLF even though they disliked the communists and were suspicious of how much control the communists had over the NLF. These intellectuals thought the Tet offensive was an indication of a more violent and widespread war in the future, and they thought the only way to save the nation was to support the NLF. They thought this because the NLF showed that regardless of the circumstances it would not be defeated, and the Tet offensive showed the US forces were not invulnerable.[22] Among many of the common people who supported the GVN the death and the destruction created by the Tet offensive intensified their hatred of the NLF, but the supporters of the NLF gained new pride because of the audacity and the bravery of the guerrillas during the offensive.[23]

A Marine in a CAP said he saw the mood of the villagers as bitter and vengeful toward the NLF after their vicious killings and the destruction of property during the Tet offensive. The villagers who were friendly toward the CAP were more open in their friendship after the offensive, and more of the people seemed friendly toward the CAP. In this Marine's opinion the Vietnamese villagers thought "Things happened that could not be forgotten."[24] In a counterinsurgency war the people may be the prize, but they suffer greatly, and this was especially true in the Vietnam War.

From Compound CAPs to Mobile CAPs

After the Tet offensive a major change was made in the way the CAPs operated. Since the start of the program in 1965, the CAPs normally established a fortified headquarters compound from which they conducted their ambush and patrol operations in the areas around the villages. The compounds were usually old buildings or abandoned fortifications located close to the villages, and the CAP members stayed in the compounds when they were not in the villages or on military operations. Sometimes, these small, isolated, and stationary positions were the target of massive attacks which overran the compounds, though, and this weakness was especially evident when a number of

CAPs were overrun during the Tet offensive. The NLF and the NVA forces were able to watch the fixed positions to find any flaws in the compound defenses, or any patterns in the habits and the schedules of the CAP members. With this information the NLF and the NVA could carefully plan their attacks and then mass their forces to attack the compounds when they thought the defenders were at their weakest. This vulnerability of the compounds to large attacks was part of the reason the Marine Corps adopted a mobile concept for the CAPs.[25]

Instead of having a compound as a headquarters, the idea of the mobile concept was to have the CAP members moving from one place to another throughout the village and the area around it. The Marines and the PFs carried all their equipment with them, and each night a different location was chosen for the CAP headquarters. During the night the CAP patrols and ambushes were conducted from this location. The next day the platoon found an area where they set out guards and slept, and later in the day the platoon patrolled in and around the village. That night the platoon chose a different position for headquarters, and patrols and ambushes were again sent out. Because they were not in a fixed position like a compound, it was more difficult for the guerrillas to find and attack the CAPs. Colonel Theodore E. Metzger commanded the CAP program during this period, and he said the NLF and the NVA "Don't like to come after you unless they've had a chance to get set and do some planning." He thought the mobile CAP concept disrupted the NLF and the NVA, though, because "Mobility throws this off.... The CAP can be found anywhere outside a village or hamlet, and they don't like this when they're trying to come in for rice, or money, or recruits, or just plain coordination."[26] The mobile CAPs "in effect" became guerrillas operating throughout their villages.

In comments he made later, Corson said he disagreed with the mobile concept because he thought the compound concept was necessary to accomplish counterinsurgency missions. He said he preferred the compound concept, and he thought the vulnerability of the compounds would not be a problem if the CAPs performed their missions correctly. Constant patrolling in and around the villages would make it more difficult for the NLF and the NVA to mass for attacks. Also, if the CAPs worked to gain the loyalty of the people then the people would give them intelligence about guerrilla activities which would prevent them from being surprised by large NLF and NVA attacks. In addition, Corson favored the compound concept because he thought the compounds were a physical expression of security in the villages, and they showed the commitment of the CAPs to the defense of the villages. The supplies for civic action projects were often kept in the compounds, and Corson thought the compounds needed to be the centers for the pacification work the CAPs conducted in the villages. When the villagers had any problems, they knew they could go to the CAP members in the compounds for help and protection. In fundamental ways this made the CAPs the social, economic, and military alternative to the NLF and in Corson's thinking they needed to be this alternative.[27]

There was considerable support for the mobile concept, though, and among the people who liked the idea was Marine Corps Master Sergeant Ralph F. Level. Level was a fascinating man who was committed to the CAP program, and he played an important part in the program for much of its existence. In 1965 he was in South Vietnam working with civic action when he transferred to the CAP organization, and from then until the program ended, he worked with the CAPs. Soon after he arrived, he began to work as an inspector of sorts as he travelled to the various CAPs to see if there were any problems with which he could help. Often, he stayed with a platoon for two or three days to watch how the CAP operated, and to talk with the men. On these occasions he evaluated the compound fortifications and he went on patrols with the platoon members to see if their patrol procedures were good. He also tried to find and resolve any problems the Marines had in their relations with the villagers and the PFs.

Throughout the time he spent with the individual CAPs, one of his primary considerations was to make sure the Marines had a good attitude toward their duty. Level thought the CAPs needed Marines who were truly sympathetic toward the Vietnamese, and who would do anything they could to help the people. When Level found a problem, he either resolved it himself, or he returned to CAP headquarters to get it resolved there.

Level acquired an excellent reputation within the entire program because of his dedication and his ability to help improve the CAPs. If the men in a platoon told him they needed something, or if something needed to be changed, he would do his best to get the problem solved. As a result of his experience, Level had a better understanding of how a successful CAP should operate than most people associated with the program, and this makes his opinions important.

In Level's opinion there were serious flaws in the compound concept. The compounds needed a great deal of work to maintain their defenses, and during the day the men were usually busy stringing barbed wire, filling sandbags, and doing other work to improve and repair the defenses of the compounds. Because of this, Level thought, there was less time for the men to perform civic action and interact with the villagers. Frequently the men were tired because they worked during the day and then went on ambush patrols at night. Living in the compounds could also create a false sense of security, in Level's opinion. Even though the compounds were fortified, they had few defenders, and they were small, isolated defensive positions. Of course, the NLF always knew where the compounds were, and they could carefully plan to attack them with a large force when and where they thought the compounds were vulnerable. For these reasons the compounds were often in danger of being overrun.

Level thought the guerrillas never knew quite where a mobile CAP might be because each mobile CAP was able to maneuver throughout its entire TAOC. This ability of the mobile CAPs to operate quickly over a wide area confused and inhibited the guerrillas. In the mobile units there was also more time for the men to sleep because they did not have to spend time working on compound defenses. During a part of the day they set out guards and slept. Later in the day they went to various hamlets in the village to perform civic action and talk with the Vietnamese people. In Level's thinking the mobile CAPs were able to conduct more counterinsurgency operations over a wider area than the compound CAPs. A Marine Corps analysis of the CAP program performance agreed with much of Level's thinking.[28]

After the CAP program was in existence for almost five years, and after the mobile CAPs were operating for approximately two years, the Marine Corps evaluated the CAP program in March 1970. Two basic reasons for the success of the CAPs were seen as their elusiveness and their unpredictability. The evaluation determined the mobile CAPs were able to use these strengths to a greater degree than the compound CAPs. The compound CAPs spent a considerable amount of time repairing and improving the defenses of the compound. Also, simply having the compound gave the platoon the disadvantage of having to use some of its men to defend a weak, fixed, defensive position, and this lessened the platoon's strength of elusiveness. Fewer ambushes were sent out because protection of the compound became the primary concern. When this happened, the guerrillas stayed away from the compound, but they were able to move more freely through the village area. The guerrillas might decide to watch the compound over a period of time and plan an assault to destroy the compound. In this way some of the compounds were overrun. However, the evaluation stated no mobile CAPs were ever destroyed. The evaluation concluded, "In pondering the relative merit of the compound CAP versus the mobile CAP, it might be well to reflect on how short this war would have been if the V.C. and the NVA operated out of fixed compounds."[29]

The evaluation explained the ambush was the most lethal tactic of the CAPs, and because of the element of surprise, an ambush could successfully engage a larger guerrilla force. If an ambush needed to disengage in a fight, the men could do it quickly, and they could often use artillery and air support to cover their withdrawal. This combination of the surprise of an ambush and the use of supporting artillery and air support made the CAPs devastating in a fight.

Corson's endorsement of the compound CAP idea is important because of his knowledge and experience, but as described above there were advantages with the mobile CAP concept. More intensive patrolling and additional intelligence might have limited the possibility of mass attacks on the compounds, but the reality was that too many compounds were attacked and overrun. Even when relief forces were available to come to the aid of a CAP compound when it was under attack, there were instances when the NLF and the NVA set up blocking positions on the most likely routes the relief forces would use. Most of the attacks occurred during the night, and in the dark it was sometimes possible for even a small guerrilla unit to stall a relief force for hours. In situations such as these the CAP compound could be destroyed before the relief force could arrive. This possibility was not as much of a concern for the mobile CAPs because they could evade most attempts by a larger force to destroy them. While the compounds may have been seen as a manifestation of CAP security for the villages, too frequently the CAP members needed to work on the defenses of the compound rather than patrolling in the village and talking with and helping the Vietnamese people. The mobile CAPS were able to interact with the people in the hamlets and on the farms as they constantly moved throughout the entire area of the villages. As they did this they let the Vietnamese people know they were there to help and protect them. In this way the mobile units showed the people they were forces which could quickly come to protect them if they were threatened by the NLF, and not defenders restricted in their movement because they were tied to a static position.

The mobile CAPs were also able to conduct more civic action over a wider area because of their freedom of movement. Often the CAPs stopped to help farmers with their work or provide medical care. At times this increased interaction with the people of the entire village area resulted in the creation of widespread intelligence networks and these networks made it possible for the CAPs to quickly respond to any NLF activity. Through their actions the mobile CAPs showed the people they were the social, economic, and military alternative to the NLF.

After Corson took command of the CAP program, he said he did not try to make all CAPs conform to one rigid model. He realized each village was a unique situation for various social, cultural, and military reasons. Rather than using a standard formula, he used the counterinsurgency principles which worked in each village, and he allowed the CAP members to chose some of the principles which they thought were appropriate for their villages. In keeping with this idea after Corson left there may have been circumstances in which a compound CAP was more appropriate than a mobile CAP, and the reverse is true, also. Having the flexibility to use either of these ideas, or modifications of either of them, made the entire CAP concept a more adaptable and effective counterinsurgency method.

Another reason for the adoption of the mobile CAP concept was related to the actions of the Civil Operations and Rural Support (CORDS) agency. In 1967, President Johnson's insistence on more emphasis on pacification led him to send Robert W. Komer to take command of an organization to coordinate all the

US pacification activities. The new organization was CORDS, and it took control of all US pacification operations including economic development, US district and village advisers to land reform, US advisory responsibility for RF and PF forces, and the elimination of the NLF infrastructure.

Komer was dynamic and aggressive in his efforts to bring all US pacification programs under the control of CORDS, and he upset many in the Marine Corps when he attempted to take control of the CAP program. Marine Corps Major General E.E. Anderson said. "When Komer was there, he tried his darndest to get the CAP program absorbed into the RF/PF program.... So, what Komer's latest ploy was, to absorb the CAPs into the RF/PF structure and that would be controlled by DepCORDs...." Anderson said to prevent this from happening Marine Corps General Cushman "Felt that by coming up with some new idea, like the mobile CAP, he would get more mileage out of the CAP program and forestall any attempt on the part of Komer ... to destroy the program."[30] So, adopting the mobile concept was seen as a way to improve CAP performance, and also as a way to help the program continue to exist as a separate command.

In the Aftermath of the TET Offensive

In March 1968, the information was made public that Westmoreland would leave his command to become the Army Chief of Staff in June, to be replaced by General Creighton W. Abrams as the commander of US forces in South Vietnam. Before assuming his new command, Abrams had served as Westmoreland's deputy commander, but he disagreed with Westmoreland's strategy of attrition and the tactics of search and destroy. Abrams agreed with the conclusions of the earlier PROVN study which stated the most important objective in the war was security for the Vietnamese people, and the strategy of attrition was contributing little if anything to accomplish that security.

After he took command Abrams began to put some of the PROVN ideas into practice with his "one war" strategy. Admiral John S. McCain, Jr. was the Commander in Chief, Pacific (CINCPAC) at this time, and during a trip to South Vietnam Abrams explained to McCain that, "The one war concept puts equal emphasis on military operations, improvement of RVNAF [Republic of Vietnam Armed Forces] and pacification—all of which are interrelated so that the better we do in one, the more our chance of progress in the others."[31] This balanced approach by Abrams was similar to a more classic counterinsurgency strategy than Westmoreland's strategy of attrition, and regarding NLF and NVA losses Abrams said, "I don't think it makes any difference how many losses he [the enemy] takes. I don't think that makes any difference."[32] Abrams' ideas in 1968 sounded different from Westmoreland's ideas, and they sounded similar to those Krulak expressed in 1965.

When Abrams was looking for someone to serve as his deputy commander, his comments revealed the intense level of inter-service rivalry between the US Army and the Marine Corps during the war. Abrams's dislike of the Marine Corps in general and Krulak in particular became evident when he was asked if he would accept Krulak as his deputy commander. He said, "In my judgement, no Marine has the full professional military qualifications to satisfactorily discharge the military responsibilities of the office." The level of Abrams's displeasure with this possibility became more evident when he said if Krulak were forced upon him as his deputy, Abrams would publicly state his opposition.[33] This inter-service rivalry between the US Army and the Marine Corps had a greater negative effect on the US war effort in the Vietnam War than most people realize.

Chapter 9

An Evaluation of the CAP Program

The CAP program continued to expand after the Tet offensive, and in 1969 the program reached its peak expansion of the Vietnam War. In 1967 the goal was to have a total of 114 CAPs operating by the end of that year. For various reasons, such as the demands made on the Marine Corps by the fighting in the DMZ area, this goal was not realized, but during 1968 twenty-three new CAPs were formed for a total of 102 platoons operating by the end of the year. In 1969 the program expansion continued until the 1967 goal of 114 operational CAPs was finally met in August 1969.[1]

After more than five years of war the CAP program, and the war itself, were very different from the beginning in 1965. Some changes were instituted to make the CAPs a better counterinsurgency force. The enemy struck, and the CAPs adjusted and countered. In other instances, the CAPs were forced to change because they were a small piece in the failing US war in South Vietnam. One of the most damaging problems for the program was Westmoreland's refusal to support the program, and his active opposition to the CAPs made it difficult for the program to operate well. The GVN made change necessary, also. For the most part the GVN was worse than inept; it worked as a hindrance to the progress of the CAPs and the best intentions of the US in South Vietnam. Examining some of the problems and successes of the CAPs can help determine whether they were an effective counterinsurgency concept in the war.

Throughout the existence of the program there were problems common to most of the CAPs which hindered the Marines. One of the most important problems for the CAP program was the inability of almost all the CAP Marines to speak the Vietnamese language. In the CAP school, the Marines received minimal Vietnamese language training, at best, and it was assumed they would learn more of the language as they worked with their platoons in the villages. In fact, though, many of the Marines in the CAPs only learned a few Vietnamese words, local slang, and a few phrases. Some of the CAPs saw this as a serious problem, and classes were conducted in which Marines taught English to the Vietnamese, and villagers taught Vietnamese to the Marines. Even some of the CAP Marines who had more extensive Vietnamese language training found it difficult to communicate with the people. In one situation a Marine assigned to a remote CAP village found his Vietnamese language training was almost useless because his instructor spoke Saigonese, and he said, "Vietnamese as spoken in Saigon is much different from what is spoken in the countryside. Out there dialects can change considerably in 10 miles."[2] In many instances any language training the CAP Marines received was useless because the villagers frequently spoke a local dialect which might also include some French, some slang terms, and possibly even some Japanese.[3]

Because so few of the CAP Marines spoke any Vietnamese, the Marines needed to find other ways to communicate with the PFs and the villagers. Often a number of the PFs and the villagers spoke some English, and this was helpful in communicating. For the most part, though, the Marines communicated with the people and the PFs through the use of hand gestures, some common Vietnamese phrases, and a form of pidgin English that evolved in many areas of Vietnam during the course of the war.[4] These forms of communication were adequate in some respects, but there were still important communication problems.

Another problem for the Marine Corps generally and the CAPs in particular in accomplishing their counterinsurgency objectives was the lack of support they received from either the GVN or the ARVN. One of the basic tenets of the counterinsurgency approach of the Marine Corps in Vietnam was that the GVN would counter the appeal of the NLF by improving the lives of the people of Vietnam. In its early attempts at pacification the Marine Corps cleared the NLF fighters from the Vietnamese villages and then gave the responsibility for pacifying the villages to the GVN and the ARVN. Neither the GVN nor the ARVN did well in these pacification efforts, and the Marine Corps concluded both these organizations were either unwilling or unable to conduct effective pacification in the villages.

While the inability and the unwillingness of many in the GVN and the ARVN to conduct pacification created problems for the Marine Corps, these problems were compounded by the widespread corruption in the GVN. Corruption was the rule rather than the exception, and this corruption put the Marine Corps in the difficult position of trying to gain the loyalty of the people for a government which did not deserve that loyalty.

If anything, the corruption and the brutality with which the ARVN treated the people were worse because the ARVN soldiers were supposedly protecting the villagers from the NLF. The ARVN troops were usually unwilling conscripts, but they often acted toward the people more as if they were part of an invading army punishing a subjected population. The people in one village said when the ARVN troops came through their village on operations the soldiers were always rude, they used excessive force, and they stole. The people said even when the soldiers were not on duty they would often stand by the road and extort money from farmers and tradesmen who passed by them. A villager showed the degree of hatred the people had for the ARVN when he described the ARVN soldiers as "Cruel like the French."[5] The people often saw the ARVN as enemies rather than protectors.

The anger and the distrust of the Vietnamese people for many in the GVN and the ARVN meant the CAPs needed to adjust how they conducted some of their counterinsurgency tasks in the villages. At the conclusion of his Phong Bac pacification experiment Corson said the CAPs needed to be prepared to protect their pacification work in the villages from any members of the NLF, the GVN, or the ARVN. Also, part of the reason Corson wanted to make the pacified villages economically independent was to keep the people from having to depend on either the GVN or the ARVN for economic help. When the CAPs performed psychological operations in the villages, they did not try to criticize the guerrillas and promote the loyalty of the people to the central government. Instead, they attempted to circumvent the anger of the people toward the GVN and the ARVN by criticizing the guerrillas and promoting the loyalty of the people to the CAPs.

In working to accomplish the counterinsurgency task of developing and strengthening the local government, the CAPs usually allowed the local governments to work on their own, but they often protected the local governments from the NLF and the corrupt influences of both the GVN and the ARVN. The CAPs did this with the intention of allowing the local governments to be strong and independent, and not with the intention of improving the control of the central government over the villages.

This created paradoxes in the villages because this meant some of the people liked the CAPs, and they frequently made friends with the Marines, but they did not like the GVN. Many of the people were in a difficult situation because they feared and hated the NLF and the NVA, but they also saw the ARVN as their enemies rather than their protectors. As a result of this the CAPs frequently gained the loyalty of the villagers, but the GVN and the ARVN did not. The glaring problem in this was that the Marines would have to leave eventually.

One of the greatest problems for the entire CAP program was that the CAPs were not positioned adjacent to each other to create one unified and constantly expanding pacified area. In counterinsurgency theory the enclave concept is meant to be used to pacify an area, and then to gradually expand the size of the pacified enclave. This was Krulak's intention when he conceived his enclave strategy. The *Small Wars Manual* stated that the location of the enclave is chosen because the region has resources the insurgents need, and the expanding enclave drives the insurgents out of the area and blocks them from the resources in the enclave. Within the enclave military forces continue to operate to eliminate any remaining insurgents.[6]

Robert Thompson gave more detail to explain the idea of the counterinsurgency enclave strategy in *Defeating Communist Insurgency*. He said the enclaves needed to expand to drive the insurgents out of the populated areas where they could obtain the food, recruits, supplies, and intelligence they needed. To make this process effective it was necessary to station troops in the villages within the enclave to keep the insurgents away from the people, and to destroy any insurgents remaining in the enclave. To keep the insurgents out of the enclave and away from the people the occupied villages needed to be adjacent to each other to form an overlapping pattern of pacified territory within the enclave. If the occupied villages were not made part of an unbroken pacified area, then the villages would be little more than isolated outposts. If this were the case the insurgents would still have access to the unoccupied villages in the areas between the occupied villages, and they would still have access to the people and the resources the insurgents needed to support their movement.[7]

The Marine Corps did not position the CAPs to create an unbroken area of mutually supporting villages, and this was a primary shortcoming of the program. This detracted from the ability of the CAP program to realize its full potential as a counterinsurgency concept. Douglas S. Blaufarb supported this conclusion in his book, *The Counterinsurgency Era*, when he said a significant problem for the CAP program was, "The failure of the command to link the various CAPs together into an interlocking and mutually supporting network. They were too scattered and isolated to have maximum impact."[8] Much of the potential of the CAP program was wasted because the CAPs were not positioned to make them part of one expanding, pacified area.

Despite the problems, the CAP program had potential. How much of this potential was realized is the question.

Security for the villages was the primary counterinsurgency task for the CAPs, and the security the CAPs provided the villages was always excellent. This was possible because the CAPs created a force with the strength of a Marine squad with a platoon of PFs who were members of the village they were defending. The majority of the Marines who served in the CAPs were volunteers with combat experience, and they were enthusiastic to fight the guerrillas. Most of the Marines were chosen for their ability and their desire to work with and defend the Vietnamese people. A key strength of the CAPs was that a Marine was transferred from the program if he did not work well with the people, or if he was inadequate in any of his other duties. The PFs in the platoon were usually poorly armed and poorly disciplined, but they were strongly motivated to protect their families and the people of the village from the NLF. They also had an intimate knowledge of the area, and they knew many of the habits and tactics of the guerrillas. By themselves the Marines would have been lost trying to fight guerrillas they could not find in a village they did not understand. By themselves the PFs were too weak to fight the guerrillas.

The meshing of these two very different groups into one platoon was possible because their common purpose was to defend the village from anyone who tried to harm the Vietnamese people. They taught each other their respective strengths, and the PFs gave the Marines a connection with the people. The result was a strong, motivated combat unit with deep emotional and cultural connections to the community it defended.

The second counterinsurgency task for the CAPs was to prevent the NLF from obtaining food, supplies, recruits, and intelligence information from the villages. This was accomplished primarily through good security measures, and this was done very well. Usually the guerrillas went into the villages at night to get what they needed, and prior to the operations of the CAPs they had little difficulty doing this. The CAP practice of setting a web of night ambushes throughout the TAOC was an excellent tactic to counter these activities. Any guerrilla movement in the night then ran the risk of running into a devastating ambush.

Gaining the goodwill and the loyalty of the Vietnamese people was an important task for the CAP program. Without this the CAPs could not have any support or cooperation from either the villagers or the PFs. This was so critical that if a Marine would not or could not do this he was transferred out of the program. Combining the Marines and the PFs into one military unit helped gain the goodwill and the loyalty of the people because they saw the two groups living and working together to protect the villagers. In addition to protection, the Marines always showed respect for the people and their culture. The CAPs also gained the loyalty of the people because of what they did not do.

The CAPs protected the Vietnamese people, and they tried to help them live better lives, but they took nothing from them.

With the protection of the CAPs the people kept all the rice they grew, and they kept the money the NLF would have taken as taxes. This protection also prevented any of the villagers from being forcibly taken to be fighters for the NLF. In the chaos of the war, the people were able to live and work in relative peace. This relationship between the CAPs and the people put the NLF at a disadvantage.

The NLF was a deeply committed insurgency which fought against real social, political, and economic injustices in South Vietnam, and for the insurgency to succeed it needed to convince the people to sacrifice in the present for the NLF promise of a better life in the future. The NLF had to convince them to think in this way because their support was crucial for the success of the insurgency. The insurgency could not exist without the protection, food, supplies, tax money, recruits, and intelligence it received from the people. This was the essential lifeline for the insurgency.

Initially the people supported the NLF as a result of commitment to its cause or because of fear of retribution, but as the war continued, the NLF increased its demands. More fighters were needed to replace casualties, and the replacements had to come from the villages. Also, more tax money, supplies, and food were needed as the ranks of the NLF increased and the violence of the war intensified. This problem was compounded for the NLF because they also had to supply many of the NVA units in South Vietnam with food. Altogether this placed an incredible burden on the Vietnamese people. If the people hesitated to give the NLF what it wanted and needed, the NLF responded with intimidation and terror.

In this competition for the goodwill and the loyalty of the people the CAPs had a distinct advantage. The CAPs took nothing from the people, and they protected them from anyone who tried to harm them. Many villagers welcomed this situation, and they were reluctant to help the NLF. Because of this the NLF responded with even more terror and intimidation. This caused many of the people to give their loyalty to the CAPs.

One of the primary counterinsurgency strengths of the CAPs was their ability to gather intelligence. As in most insurgencies, the NLF had an advantage in acquiring intelligence because its supporters among the Vietnamese people could watch almost every move the Marine and the ARVN forces made, and then report this information to the guerrillas. For various reasons including their fear of retribution from the NLF and their hatred of the soldiers, some of the Vietnamese civilians were frequently reluctant to give the Marine and ARVN infantry units intelligence information. In his book, *Isolating the Guerillas*, Michael F. Trevett pointed out an additional problem for the Marines and the ARVN in their efforts to gather intelligence. He said, "The predicament of the counterguerrilla forces is compounded by the fact that conventional intelligence sections of military units, trained to gather and process combat intelligence, are normally neither prepared nor manned to gather and process information on hundreds of individuals."[9] Because they lived and operated among the people in the villages, the Marines and the PFs in the CAPs were usually aware of the general attitudes of the people, and they were uniquely capable of obtaining information related to all NLF activities in their areas. Also, the CAP members learned a great deal about many of the villagers among whom they lived, and they were able to provide the military intelligence units with all this important information. This familiarity with the people and their knowledge of the areas in which they operated made the CAPs a uniquely valuable asset for the intelligence-gathering functions of the military intelligence units.

The NLF infrastructure members were part of the social, political, and economic structure the NLF established to replace government organizations and to enforce its control of the villages. One of the responsibilities of these agents was to ensure the guerrillas were supplied with what they needed. Some of these people were well-hidden within the society of the villages, and very few if any of the people knew who they were. The activities of the CAPs made it difficult for these agents to operate, though.

Eliminating the NLF infrastructure in the villages was a difficult task, but the CAPs did a good job of limiting their activities. Some of these agents were found, but even when they were not detected the constant surveillance and patrolling of the area by the CAP platoon made their jobs more dangerous. Intelligence sources among the people were also able to discover who some of these agents were and they reported this information to the CAPs. It was virtually impossible to find all the infrastructure members from the villages, but the CAPs were able to find some of them, and the threat of discovery made it dangerous for them to contact and supply the guerrillas.

The best civic action projects the CAPs completed in the villages were small, basic improvements, but they helped improve the quality of life for the entire community. Living through years of war was difficult for the people, and conditions in the villages deteriorated. Many of the CAPs dug wells, put irrigation pumps in rice paddies, and repaired bridges, schools, and other village buildings. At times Marines or PFs in a platoon had a background in carpentry, or some other skill, and they used their skills to help with civic action projects.

The most helpful element of the civic program was undoubtedly the medical care the corpsmen gave the people. The people in the villages were terribly neglected in respect to medical care, and the corpsmen's medical care became the most valued feature of civic action. In addition to the care the corpsmen gave in the villages, serious medical cases were transported to hospitals by helicopters.

The civic action projects and the medical care brought real improvements to the people's lives. They were also another way the CAPs showed the people they were dedicated to helping them.

Economic development was similar to civic action in that it usually consisted of small projects which helped the entire community. Just as with civic action, at times a Marine in a CAP might have experience in farming, and he could suggest a new crop the villagers could plant, or animals they could raise. On some occasions the CAP members helped the farmers with their work.

The greatest improvements to the economic circumstances of the villages were a result of the CAPs keeping the NLF, the ARVN, and US military forces away from the villages. With the CAPs protecting the villages it was much more difficult for the NLF to extort tax money and rice from the people, and this improved the economic situation considerably. CAP protection also meant ARVN troops could no longer come through the villages and steal from the people, as they usually did. US military units were not able to move through the area without good reason, either. This was a benefit for the villages because the US forces often had tanks and other armored vehicles which would damage the bridges and drive through the rice paddies. The people were also more productive because they were able to work in relative peace without having their lives disrupted by the worst violence of the war.

The CAPs did an excellent job in the areas of civic action and economic development. The projects in both these areas were often small, but they brought real improvements to the villages. Also, the greatest civic action and economic development improvements were accomplished by keeping the NLF, the ARVN, and the US military units away from the villages.

The CAPs always did well in their psychological operations counterinsurgency task. The goal of the psychological operations was to discredit the guerrillas and to promote the loyalty of the people to the CAPs, and they did a good job of this. The CAPs made a point of treating the people with respect and kindness, and they provided excellent security for the villagers, and these were the two most important elements of the psychological operations to gain people's loyalty. Many of the people appreciated the CAP members for treating them well, and because of this some of them gave the Marines and the PFs their friendship. The CAPs were also able to fight and defeat the guerrillas to keep them away from the villages, and this meant the guerrillas were no longer able to take taxes, recruits, and rice from the people. Because of this many people were loyal to the CAPs and respected the platoon members. To gain the loyalty of the people the CAPs continued to treat them well, and they made sure the people knew they were defeating the guerrillas.

The CAPs were doing a good job of accomplishing the counterinsurgency task of developing and strengthening the local government. The local governments in the Vietnamese villages were controlled by the village families and the councils of elders, and the Marines were usually prudent enough to allow the local governments to function without their interference. The CAPs respected the authority of the local governments, and they helped them when their help was needed. The security provided for the villages also played an important part in strengthening the local governments because the CAPs protected the local governments from both the NLF and corrupt elements of the GVN.

While the CAPs were working to develop and strengthen the local governments, they were doing little to accomplish the counterinsurgency task of improving the control of the GVN over the villages. In an attempt to increase respect for the GVN among the people, the CAPs made numerous requests for GVN help with pacification work in the villages, but in almost every instance the GVN was either unable or unwilling to provide this help.[10] In addition to this, many of the GVN officials were corrupt and inattentive to the needs of the people. For these reasons many of the Vietnamese hated and feared the GVN, and they wanted to have as little as possible to do with the government. Many of the Marines in the CAPs knew the people hated the GVN because of its corruption, and they would often protect the people from the GVN officials as well as the NLF.

The hatred of many of the Vietnamese toward the GVN looked as if it was an insurmountable problem which made the war unwinnable. After the war a former NVA officer said, "The South Vietnamese government was originally a French creation set up in the context of a colonial war of reconquest." As a result of this, many Vietnamese saw GVN leaders as "Figures from the colonial past." The former officer saw this lack of credibility as a crucial problem for the GVN and he said, "This fundamental weakness was beyond the ability of the United States to correct." This problem was increased because "The nepotism and feudal bureaucracy of the Diem administration, and the many *coups d' etat* that followed Diem's overthrow, led by generals all trained and raised to leadership positions by the French, made this weakness even more glaring."[11] Problems such as these suggest the entire US war effort was an impossible task in support of an illegitimate government.

The CAPs were a successful counterinsurgency concept in the Vietnam War, and their success was elegant in its simplicity. The fundamental reasons for their success were that they treated the people with kindness and respect, they took nothing from them, and they protected them from anyone who threatened to harm them. The common goal of protecting the people made it possible to combine the strength of a Marine squad with the PFs who had knowledge of the area and cultural connections to the villagers.

The CAPs did not accomplish the counterinsurgency task of improving the control of the central government over the villages. This was not done because the GVN was simply an illegitimate government. The war was a reality, though, and the CAPs chose to defend the villages from the GVN, the NLF, and anyone else who threatened the people. As they did this, their protection allowed the local governments to develop and grow stronger, Because of this many of the hamlets were able to achieve the traditional goal of becoming independent. This was certainly a moral success for the CAPs. This was a principled stand on the part of the men who served in the CAPs, and it speaks well for their collective character.

These were some of the reasons the CAPs were a successful counterinsurgency concept, but there was another reason. The CAPs accomplished the most challenging and necessary counterinsurgency goal of separating the insurgents from what they needed most. In any insurgency, the guerrillas depend on the people for food, supplies, recruits, and the intelligence they need to maintain the insurgency. The NLF was not an exception to this rule, and they depended on the Vietnamese villages to provide them with all of this. This was the jugular vein of the insurgency, and the CAPs effectively cut it. From an overall perspective, this was the greatest accomplishment of the CAP program. The CAPs were only allowed to do this on a limited scale, though, and the opportunity to use this successful counterinsurgency method more widely was squandered.

The End of an Experiment

In 1969 President Richard M. Nixon changed the Vietnam War dramatically with the introduction of the policy of Vietnamization. The war seemed as if it was a never-ending nightmare for the United States, and Nixon later wrote, "It was no longer a question of whether the next President would withdraw our troops but of how they would leave and what they would leave behind."[12] The intention of this new policy was to give the South Vietnamese the responsibility of fighting the war while the United States continued to provide monetary and material support. Nixon told General Abrams that the principal mission of US troops was now to help the military forces of the GVN become capable of fighting the war without the assistance of US ground forces. The US was withdrawing its troops from South Vietnam, and a core part of the new mission was to train the GVN military forces to be able to fight the war on their own when the US troops were gone.[13]

The policy of Vietnamization meant the focus of the CAP program would now be the training of GVN military forces to make them capable of fighting on their own. In 1967 Krulak, Walt, and Nickerson gave the CAP program the mission of pacifying the Vietnamese villages because they thought the GVN forces were not willing or able to do the work. As a consequence of this shift in US policy to Vietnamization, a major portion of the CAP program's effort was now to train the PFs to defend their villages when the Marines left. The individual CAPs trained their PFs, and PF and RF platoons were often brought to CAG locations for an accelerated training course before they returned to their villages and their regions.[14]

As the Marine Corps began its withdrawal from Vietnam in July 1969, this increased emphasis on training led to the creation of units similar to the CAPs but used almost exclusively for training the PFs and the RFs. In October 1969 the Infantry Company Intensive Pacification Program (ICIPP) was initiated to use US Army and Marine Corps infantry companies to train the PFs and the RFs. Altogether, two US Army infantry companies and three US Marine Corps infantry companies participated in this program, which was later designated as the Combined Unit Pacification Program (CUPP). The men in these infantry units received little if any special training for their mission, but they lived in the villages and provided security. Unlike the CAPs, the CUPPs were formed to give the PFs and the RFs as much training as possible before the US completely withdrew its forces.[15]

The use of the CAP concept as a method of counterinsurgency pacification in the Vietnamese villages had ended, and the CAPs were being disbanded as US forces withdrew from Vietnam. Until they were disbanded, the focus of the CAP Marines was on providing security in their villages and training the PFs and the RFs to fight the NLF and the NVA after the Marines were gone.

In July 1969 the Third Marine Division left Vietnam and returned to Okinawa. CAP units continued to be deactivated in Vietnam as the Marine Corps withdrew more of its forces. The end of the CAP program was on May 17, 1971, when the last CAPs were deactivated. This marked the end of the United States Marine Corps Combined Action Platoons in the Vietnam War.

Conclusion

This study examines whether the CAP concept developed by the US Marine Corps was an effective counterinsurgency concept in the Vietnam War. The CAP program was evaluated according to its ability to perform a number of fundamental counterinsurgency tasks within the context of the Vietnam War. The CAPs performed some of these tasks in an exceptional manner, and they performed all but one of the remaining tasks well. The total counterinsurgency effect of the CAPs was superb. The CAP program had great potential as a counterinsurgency concept, but for various reasons most of this potential was never realized. Among the most important of these reasons were the conflict between the US Army and the US Marine Corps over the best strategy for the war, and the corruption and the illegitimacy of the GVN. For these and other reasons the CAP program was an excellent counterinsurgency concept which was used neither intelligently enough, nor extensively enough, in the Vietnam War.

At times in history the actions of one person can contribute to success in difficult circumstances. Unfortunately, the reverse of this is also true, and the actions of one person can help ruin a promising situation. At other times even the best ideas of people can be frustrated so the result is failure. In the history of the CAP concept as a counterinsurgency method in the Vietnam War, Generals William Westmoreland and Victor Krulak, and Lt. Col. William Corson were three men who significantly influenced the CAP program.

Westmoreland was the MACV commander, and it was his responsibility to select the military strategy for the war. He chose a strategy of attrition, and this aggressive strategy to destroy the main force units of the NVA and the NLF made some sense in 1965. The momentum of the large enemy units needed to be blunted and sending US battalions and regiments to find and destroy them was a good way to counter their actions. However, as the enemy began to adjust to the tactics of search and destroy, the US needed to adjust strategy and tactics, also.

The arguments Krulak made for the adoption of an enclave strategy were reasoned and based on compelling evidence. There were also others who opposed the strategy of attrition and the tactics of search and destroy. Among those were the people who conducted the PROVN study, and those who agreed with its conclusions. Even if Westmoreland did not want to adopt the enclave strategy, he should have seen the need for a change in strategy and tactics. His failure to do this implies he had too much pride, too little intellectual vision, or too little courage to make the change.

As a part of the enclave strategy, the CAP program suffered because of a lack of support from the Army. Westmoreland refused to allow the Marine Corps to allocate additional men to the program, and he pushed the Marine Corps to use its men in search and destroy operations rather than in pacification programs. A more logical approach might have been to see the enclave strategy and the CAP program concept in I Corps as an experimental strategy to observe. Part of Westmoreland's reason for opposing the enclave strategy and the CAP program may have been that he was blinded by the intense rivalry between the Army and the Marine Corps.

The CAP program was given its greatest opportunity to achieve success as a counterinsurgency concept when Corson was given the CAP program as a separate command. Very simply, he seemed to be the right man, in the right place, at the right time. His expertise, his experience, and his charisma made him an excellent choice for the job, and he did it well. The Phong Bac experiment developed important principles which were used in the CAP program. His initial organization, selection, and training for the program were fine. In practice, though, his plan experienced problems.

Some of the problems for the CAP program as a separate command were beyond Corson's control. Corson attempted to get the authorization he needed to expand the successful CAP program, but he was never given this permission. This contributed to the inability of the program to realize its full potential as a counterinsurgency concept. The NVA attacks in the DMZ and surrounding area were problems which greatly affected the CAP program, and these were also beyond Corson's control. Those attacks drew Marine Corps resources away from pacification in the coastal areas of I Corps, as they were intended to do, and this meant there were fewer resources available to support the CAP program.

One of the most important questions in the history of the CAPs is why Corson left the program after commanding it for only a few months. He saw the counterinsurgency potential of the program, and under his command it was developing well. This seemed to be an opportunity for him to use his experience and his knowledge to make a decisive contribution to the war. It is difficult to determine why people do what they do, though. However, a military unit takes on some of the personality traits of its commander, and if he had stayed longer the story would have been better.

These three men had a great influence on the CAP program in various ways, but in the end the program needs to be judged by its performance. The two great strengths of the CAPs were their ability to provide security for the villages and to gather useful intelligence. They accomplished these two tasks very well. No village in which a CAP was located was ever reoccupied by the NLF or the NVA. Some CAPs were overrun, but the Marines and the PFs soon reestablished the CAPs and took control again. The CAPs were also an excellent source of intelligence. They were considered to be among the best sources of intelligence in many of the areas where they were located. These were their two greatest strengths.

The psychological operations of the CAPs were very good, also. This was made easier for the CAPs because their actions spoke for them. They defeated the guerrillas and kept them out of the villages. This proved the CAPs would protect the people from the NLF. Also, they treated the people well, and they took nothing from them. This was the essence of their psychological operations message. Because of these actions they disproved NLF propaganda which claimed the Marines would abuse the people.

The CAPs did well in accomplishing the intelligence-related task of finding and eliminating the hidden members of the NLF infrastructure among the villagers. Finding these hidden agents was important, because if they continued to operate in the villages, they could send intelligence to the guerrillas, and they could target any villagers who cooperated with the CAPs for reprisal. Some of these agents were discovered, and the activities of others were inhibited by the patrols and the intelligence operations of the CAPs. The NLF received less rice and fewer recruits from the CAP villages, and this was proof the infrastructures were weakened.

In the areas of civic action and economic development, the CAPs did a good job of accomplishing these tasks. The small, practical projects brought real improvements to the lives of the villagers, and the corpsmen's medical care was especially well-received. Protecting the villages from the NLF and others allowed the people to keep their money and the food they produced. This protection helped the village economies a great deal.

The CAPs helped develop and strengthen the local governments, but they did little to improve the control of the central government over the villages. Most of the CAPs wisely let the local governments operate in their traditional manner, and the security the CAPs gave the villages made it possible for the local governments to function in a stable atmosphere without NLF interference. Helping the GVN improve its control over the villages was a problem, though, because the GVN was almost always unwilling or unable to help with the CAP pacification work. This situation was further complicated because many of the villagers hated and distrusted the GVN because they saw the government as illegitimate, and the government officials frequently exploited the people in various ways.

The CAP program was not given adequate support as a counterinsurgency concept during the Vietnam War, and the leadership of the program was responsible for some of this failure. In too many instances the men did not have enough of their most basic needs such as food, clothing, ammunition, and radios. This was a problem which should have been resolved by the CAP command. Also, there should not have been a shortage of men for the CAPs. Many Marines in Vietnam who were not in the infantry would have volunteered for the CAP program if they were given the opportunity. The training in the CAP school would have prepared them for duty in the CAPs. In 1967 the program was opened for men who did not have an infantry background, but if this were done earlier there would have been more men available for the CAPs.

These were problems which should have been resolved by the CAP command. This evaluation needs to be qualified, though. The war placed conflicting demands and immense pressure on the leaders of the program, and in many ways the war was as confusing for the commanders as it was for the junior officers and the enlisted men. To evaluate the problem fairly more research might show why the CAP program was not given more support.

There are other areas where additional historical research would be rewarding. The CAPs brought together people from at least two very different cultures in the turbulent and stressful setting of a war, and a cultural study of the CAPs might lead to a more nuanced understanding of the program. Another area for further study might be Lt. Colonel William Corson. At times in this study Corson appeared as if he was a Renaissance man in a tragedy. After a career of primarily clandestine service, Corson was given the mission of using his accumulated knowledge of counterinsurgency to form the CAP program. Corson abruptly left his new command after only a few months, and why he left is puzzling, A study of Corson's military career would be a valuable addition to the study of the CAPs, and a valuable addition to the study of US military history.

Still, the idea of the CAPs is intriguing, and some have said if the concept had been used more widely in the Vietnam War, an outcome more favorable to the US could have been achieved. Many see the CAPs as an excellent method of counterinsurgency pacification. The CAPs fought the guerrillas during the night and helped the villagers during the day. Much of this was true, of course, and after observing the CAPs William Lederer wrote the CAP program was "Our one successful effort. It should be spread to every corner of rural Vietnam."[1] In considering the results of using units such as the CAPs in a widespread manner, Robert B. Asprey wrote, "Had the pacification process developed in a qualitative, orderly, and intelligent manner, the enemy probably would have attacked in force and been flattened by unquestionably superior firepower."[2]

It is impossible to know what might have happened, but as Corson said, "And for the first time since we have confronted a war of national liberation, we know how to defeat the Communists in an insurgency environment." Very simply, the CAPs were defeating the NLF in the villages. The platoons controlled the villages, and they gained the loyalty of many of the people. Their successful tactics kept the guerrillas away from the villages and blocked the NLF from the rice they needed to feed both themselves and the NVA. The NLF was also prevented from getting recruits and intelligence from the villages. The CAPs worked well in their villages, and it is reasonable to conclude they would have worked well in other villages within enclaves. It is also reasonable to conclude the CAPs were a successful counterinsurgency concept in the Vietnam War, and the program was not given enough support to allow it to realize its full potential.

A good deal of this study has looked at the conflicting strategies and tactics of the US military in the Vietnam War to determine whether or not the CAPs were an effective counterinsurgency concept in the war, and why they were or were not effective in the war. The conclusion is that the CAPs were an effective concept, but many of the problems of the CAPs were related to the problems experienced by the entire US military. Douglas Porch summarized the problems well when he wrote, "The real problem was the political and strategic context in which the war was fought." He said no combination of strategy and tactics could overcome the problem of "A corrupt and illegitimate South Vietnamese military." This problem was compounded because the US and its allies confronted "An enemy who enjoyed an inviolate sanctuary, nationalist legitimacy, solid political and military leadership, a motivated and adaptable military force, a command economy, and two powerful communist allies who supplied … virtually unlimited *materiel*."[3] The problem was not a question of the correct strategy and tactics for the US because the Vietnam War was unwinnable.

This is a popular evaluation of the war, but after the war began it was the responsibility of military commanders to help achieve the best possible outcome for the US, and for the people of South Vietnam. Within the existing enclaves, the CAP platoons controlled the villages. In effect, this meant the people in the villages were able to live their lives free of GVN and ARVN interference. Krulak's strategic plan included enclaves to protect South Vietnam's primary rice-growing regions in northeastern South Vietnam and in the Mekong Delta. If CAPs within the villages of these enclaves protected the people from government corruption and army brutality, the GVN and the ARVN would have been prevented from interfering in a strategic plan which helped the people of South Vietnam.

The North Vietnamese and the National Liberation Front were powerful opponents, but they had their weaknesses. The NVA and the NLF needed rice from the northeastern region of South Vietnam and the Mekong Delta. If they were blocked from getting this rice, they would have been forced to bring food down the trails from North Vietnam. This may have been possible, but they would not have been able to bring as many arms and supplies from North Vietnam because of this. If the US had made a priority of establishing CAPs in strongly defended enclaves in both the northeastern region of South Vietnam and the Mekong Delta, the combat effectiveness of the NVA and the NLF would have been lessened considerably.

The NVA and the NLF would still have been serious opponents, but they would have been deprived of much of what they needed to fight the war, including rice. Also, they would have had fewer supplies and weapons because food would have to be brought from the North. Blocking NLF access to the enclaves would have kept the NLF from the rice, the recruits, and the intelligence they needed. Making the enclaves a priority in a strategic plan such as this would have struck at the weaknesses of the NVA and the NLF. This would have made the war a much different proposition for the US.

The war was unwinnable, but the US needed to make the best of a difficult situation after the war started. Krulak's plan had the potential to achieve a better outcome for the US, and for those people in South Vietnam who did not want to live under an authoritarian, communist government.

The CAP concept was a carefully chosen and appropriate counterinsurgency method, and it was at least one of the most promising concepts for the US in the Vietnam War. It is surprising it succeeded as well as it did. It rarely received adequate supplies, and few people truly saw its value during the entire war. Also, it was opposed by some of the most powerful people in the US military and the US government. Still, it succeeded in the small area where it operated, and the potential of the CAPs as a counterinsurgency concept in the Vietnam War in general was squandered.

The CAPs were an effective counterinsurgency concept in the Vietnam War, and most of the Marines who served in the CAPs did so in an exemplary manner. Almost all of them were young men who volunteered for a dangerous assignment with the knowledge they were protecting the Vietnamese people from the NLF and the NVA. They committed themselves to the defense of the people in the villages, and many of them died in defense of their commitment. The cause for which they fought was just, and their personal commitment was honorable. The history of the CAPs is a distinguished chapter in the history of the United States Marine Corps.

Endnotes

Introduction

1. Jack Shulimson, *US Marines in Vietnam: An Expanding War, 1966* (Washington, D.C.: History and Museums Division, Headquarters, US Marine Corps, 1982), 242–243.
2. F.J. West, Jr., *The Village* (New York: Harper & Row, 1972), x.
3. Ibid., 132–133.
4. Shulimson, 1966, 243.
5. Victor H. Krulak, *First to Fight: An Inside View of the US Marine Corps* (Annapolis: Naval Institute Press, 1984), 188–189.
6. Russell F. Weigley, *The American Way of War: A History of United States Military Strategy and Policy* (Bloomington: Indiana University Press, 1973), xvii
7. Robert Dallek, *Flawed Giant: Lyndon Johnson and His Times, 1961–1973* (New York: Oxford University Press, 1998), 101.
8. Weigley, xvii.
9. Michael F. Trevett, *Isolating the Guerrilla* (Mustang, OK: Tate Publishing & Enterprises, 2011), 179–180.
10. 24 Mao Zedong, *On Guerrilla Warfare* (Urbana: University of Illinois Press, 2000), 43.
11. Ibid., 92–93.
12. Ibid., 7.
13. Vo Nguyen Giap, *People's War, People's Army* (New York: Praeger, 1971), 103–104.
14. Robert Thompson, *No Exit from Vietnam* (New York: David McKay Company, 1970), 46–48.
15. Ibid., 52.

16. John A. Nagl, *Learning to Eat Soup With a Knife* (Chicago: The University of Chicago Press, 2002), 28.
17. Bernard B. Fall, *Street Without Joy* (Mechanicsburg, PA: Stackpole Books, 1964), 374–375.
18. Nagl, 28–29.
19. Douglas Porch, *Counterinsurgency: Exposing the Myths of the New Way of War* (New York: Cambridge University Press, 2013), 327–328.
20. David Galula, *Counterinsurgency Warfare: Theory and Practice* (Westport: Praeger, 2006), viii.
21. William C. Westmoreland, *A Soldier Reports* (New York: Da Capo Press, 1989), 153.
22. Lewis Sorley, *Westmoreland: The General Who Lost Vietnam* (New York: Houghton Mifflin Harcourt, 2011), 92.
23. Ibid., 196–198.
24. John Prados, *The Journal of Military History* 63, no. 2 (Apr. 1999): 497.

Chapter 1

1. Nguyen Cao Ky, *Buddha's Child* (New York: St. Martin's Press, 2002), 144.
2. John Prados, *Vietnam: The History of an Unwinnable War, 1945–1975* (Lawrence: University Press of Kansas, 2009), 74–75.
3. Jack Shulimson and Major Charles M. Johnson, *US Marines in Vietnam, The Landing and the Buildup, 1965* (History and Museums Division Headquarters, US Marine Corps: Washington, D.C., 1978), xiii.
4. William C. Westmoreland, *A Soldier Reports* (Garden City, NY: New American Library, 1976), 139.
5. Ibid., 101.
6. Bui Tin, *From Enemy to Friend: A North Vietnamese Perspective on the War* (Annapolis: Naval Institute Press, 2002), 16–17.

7. Ibid., 16–17.
8. Ibid., 59.
9. Larry E. Cable, *A Conflict of Myths: The Development or American Counterinsurgency Doctrine and the Vietnam War* (New York: New York University Press, 1986), 186.
10. Truong Nhu Tang, *A Viet Cong Memoir: An Inside Account of the Vietnam War and its Aftermath* (New York: Vintage Books, 1986), 71.
11. Philip Caputo, *A Rumor of War* (New York: Holt, Rinehart and Winston, 1977), 27–28.
12. Ibid., 60.
13. Westmoreland, 140.
14. Caputo, 95.
15. Ibid., 74.
16. Westmoreland, 145.
17. Ibid., 145–146.
18. Ibid, 153.
19. Ibid. 152.
20. Russell F. Weigley, *The American Way of War: A History of United States Military Strategy and Policy* (Bloomington: Indiana University Press), 464–465.
21. Westmoreland, 157.
22. Lewis Sorley, *Westmoreland: The General Who Lost Vietnam* (New York: Houghton, Mifflin, Harcourt, 2011), 92–93.
23. Ibid., 93.
24. Bui Tin, 94.
25. Igor Bobrowsky interview, September 11, 1984, Klyman Collection, Folder 7, Box 1, United States Marine Corps Historical Center, Quantico, VA.
26. Al Santoli, *Everything We Had* (New York: Balantine Books, 1981), 177.
27. Lewis W. Walt, *Strange War, Strange Strategy* (New York: Funk & Wagnalls, 1970), 29.
28. Victor H. Krulak, *First to Fight: An Inside View of the U.S. Marine Corps* (Annapolis: Naval Institute Press, 1984), 197.

29. Robert Coram, *Brute: The Life of Victor Krulak, US Marine* (New York: Little, Brown and Company, 2010.), 72.
30. Ibid., 179.
31. Neil Sheehan, *A Bright Shining Lie: John Paul Vann and America in Vietnam* (New York: Random House, 1988.), 293, 297–298.
32. Krulak, *First to Fight*,180.
33. Ibid., 180, 182.
34. Victor H. Krulak, "A Strategic Concept for the Republic of Vietnam, June 1965," Klyman Collection, Box #1, US Marine Corps Archives and Special Collections, Quantico, VA.
35. Ibid.
36. Ibid.
37. Ibid.
38. Ibid.
39. Krulak, *First to Fight*, 186.
40. Ibid., 186.

Chapter 2

1. Shulimson and Johnson, 46.
2. Westmoreland, 166.
3. Shulimson and Johnson, 48, 179.
4. Ibid., 138.
5. Ibid., 38–39.
6. Capt. Lionel Silva, interview by MSC, Quantico, February 2, 1966, No. 37, Oral History Collection, US Marine Corps Archives and Special Collections, Quantico, VA.
7. Shulimson and Johnson, 39.
8. Krulak, *First to Fight*, 185.
9. Shulimson and Johnson, 47.
10. Ibid., 138–141.
11. Ibid., 141–142.

12. Ibid., 144–146
13. Ibid.
14. Krulak. *First to Fight*, 187.
15. Bruce C. Allnut, *Marine Combined Action Capabilities: The Vietnam Experience* (McLean, VA: HumanSciences Research, Inc., 1969), 8–9.
16. Shulimson and Johnson, 133, 135.
17. Paul R. Ek, interview by Jack Shulimson, November 2, 1972, Klyman collection, file 4, Box 1, US Marine Corps Archives and Special Collections, Quantico, VA.
18. Ibid.
19. Ibid.
20. Paul R. Ek, interview, Camp Pendleton, CA, February 10, 1966, No. 46, Oral History Collection, US Marine Corps Archives and Special Collections, Quantico, VA.
21. Michael A. Hennessy, *Strategy in Vietnam: The Marines and Revolutionary Warfare in I Corps, 1965–1972* (Westport: Praeger Publishers, 1997), 115.
22. Ek, interview, February 10, 1966.
23. Igor Bobrowsky interview, Klyman Collection, folder 7, Box #1. US Marine Corps Archives and Special Collections, Quantico, VA.
24. Ek interview, February 10, 1966.
25. Ibid.
26. Shulimson and Johnson, 137.
27. Ek interview, February 10, 1966.
28. Shulimson and Johnson, 136.
29. Al Hemingway, *Our War Was Different: Marine Combined Action Platoons in Vietnam* (Annapolis: Naval Institute Press, 1994), 22–23.
30. Ibid., 24–27.
31. Russell H. Stolfi, *US Marine Corps Civic Action Effort in Vietnam, March 1965–March 1966* (Washington, D.C.: Historical Branch, Headquarters US Marine Corps.), 1.

Chapter 3

1. Robert Thompson, *No Exit from Vietnam* (New York: David McKay Company, 1970), 33.
2. Jack Shulimson and Major Charles M. Johnson, *U.S. Marines in Vietnam: The Landing and the Buildup,1965* (Washington, D.C.: History and Museums Division, Headquarters, US Marine Corps, 1978), 138.
3. Philip Caputo, *A Rumor of War* (New York: Holt, Rinehart and Winston, 1977), xii.
4. James W. Trullinger, *Village at War: An Account of Conflict in Vietnam* (Stanford: Stanford University Press, 1994), 119.
5. William R. Corson, *The Betrayal* (New York: Ace Books, Inc., 1968), 193.
6. Krulak, 190.
7. Larry E. Cable, *A Conflict of Myths: The Development of American Counterinsurgency Doctrine and the Vietnam War* (New York: New York University Press, 1986), 107.
8. Allan R. Millett, *Semper Fidelis: The History of the United States Marine Corps* (New York: The Free Press, 1991), 261–263.
9. Headquarters, Marine Corps, *Small Wars Manual, United States Marine Corps, 1940* (Washington, D.C.: US Government Printing Office, 1940), 71.
10. Ibid., 419.
11. Burke Davis, *Marine!: The Life of Chesty Puller* (Boston: Little Brown and Co., 1962), 86–87.
12. Shulimson and Johnson, *US Marines in Vietnam, 1965*, 134.
13. Krulak, 190.
14. Ibid., 138.
15. Trullinger, 118.

16. Gregory A. Daddis, *Westmoreland's War: Reassessing American Strategy in Vietnam* (New York: Oxford University Press, 2014), 80.
17. Westmoreland, *A Soldier Reports*, 99–100.
18. Westmoreland, *A Soldier Reports*, 166.
19. Corson, *The Betrayal*, 178.
20. Victor H. Krulak, "A Strategic Appraisal, Vietnam December 1965," Klyman Collection, Box #1. US Marine Corps Archives and Special Collections, Quantico, VA.
21. Ibid.
22. Ibid.
23. Ibid.
24. Krulak, *First to Fight*, 199–200.
25. The Military History Institute of Vietnam, *Victory in Vietnam, the Official History of the People's Army of Vietnam, 1954–1975*, trans. Merle L. Pribbenow (Lawrence: The University Press of Kansas, 2002), xxi.
26. Bui Tin, 40–41.
27. Krulak, *First to Fight*, 199–200, 201.
28. Hemingway, p. 22.
29. John C. McManus, *Grunts: Inside the American Infantry Combat Experience, World War II through Iraq* (New York: New American Library, 2010), 220–221.

Chapter 4

1. Bruce C. Allnut, *Marine Combined Action Capabilities: The Vietnam Experience* (McLean, VA: Human Sciences Research, Inc., 1969), C-1.
2. McManus, 215–216.
3. Ibid., 216–217.
4. Ibid., 217.
5. Allnutt, 12.
6. Shulimson, 1966, 245

7. Allnutt, 35.
8. Ibid., C-5-C-6.
9. Ibid., C-6
10. Ibid.
11. McManus, 226–227.
12. Alnutt, 31.
13. Ibid., 32.
14. Ibid., E-9.
15. F.J. West, Jr., *The Village* (New York: Harper & Row, 1972), 62.
16. Allnutt, 33.
17. Ibid., 35.
18. F.J. West, 19.
19. Allnutt, 36
20. Ibid., 36–37.
21. Ibid., 38–39.
22. John A. Nagl, *Learning to Eat Soup With a Knife: Counterinsurgency Lessons from Malaya and Vietnam* (Chicago: The University of Chicago Press, 2002), xiv.
23. Allnut, 41–42.
24. Ibid., 47.
25. Hemingway, 28.
26. Ibid., 48.
27. Ibid., 62.
28. William J. Lederer, *Our Own Worst Enemy* (New York: W.W. Norton & Co., 1968), 156
29. Klyman, 18–19.
30. Geoffrey C. Ward and Ken Burns, The Vietnam War: An Intimate History (New York: Alfred A Knopf, 2017) 168–172.
31. Michael E. Peterson, *The Combined Action Platoons: The US Marines' Other War in Vietnam* (NewYork: Praeger, 1989), 31–32.
32. Shulimson, 1966, 312.

33. Ibid.
34. *The Marines in Vietnam, 1954–1973: An Anthology and Annotated Bibliography* (Washington, D.C.: History and Museums Division, Headquarters, US Marine Corps, 1985), 97.
35. Tran Ngoc Chau, *Vietnam Labyrinth: Allies, Enemies, and Why the US Lost the War* (Lubbock: Texas Tech University Press, 2012), 267.

Chapter 5

1. Victor H. Krulak to Robert S. McNamara, letter, May 9, 1966, Klyman collection, US Marine CorpsArchives and Special Collections, Quantico, Va.
2. Ibid.
3. Victor H. Krulak to Paul H. Nitze, letter, July 17, 1966, Klyman collection, US Marine Corps Archives and Special Collections, Quantico, Va.
4. Ibid.
5. Ibid.
6. John A. Nagl, *Learning to Eat Soup With a Knife: Counterinsurgency Lessons from Malaya and Vietnam* (Chicago: The University of Chicago Press, 2002), 159.
7. Ibid., 160.
8. William R. Corson, interview Russ Martin, July, 1976, transcript, US Marine Corps Archives and Special Collections, Quantico, Va.
9. Ibid.
10. William R. Corson, "Phong Bac Hamlet: Case Study in Pacification" 1967, transcript, US Marine Corps Archives and Special Collections, Quantico, Va.
11. William R. Corson, *The Betrayal* (New York: Ace Books, Inc., 1968), 163–164.
12. Ibid., 164.
13. Corson, "Phong Bac Hamlet."

14. Corson, *The Betrayal*, 168–169.
15. Willliam Lederer, *Our Own Worst Enemy* (New York: W.W. Norton, 1968), 176.
16. Ibid., 178–179.
17. Ibid., 179–180.
18. Ibid., 182–183.
19. Ibid., 183–184.
20. Ibid., 184.
21. Ibid., 185.
22. Ibid., 185–186.
23. Ibid., 179–180.
24. Michael F. Trevett, *Isolating the Guerrilla* (Mustang, OK: Tate Publishing, 2011), 141.

Chapter 6

1. William R. Corson, *The Betrayal* (New York: Ace Books, 1968), 179–180.
2. Ibid., 179.
3. Jack Shulimson, *US Marines in Vietnam: an Expanding War, 1966* (History and Museums Division, Headquarters, US Marine Corps: Washington, D.C., 1978), 239.
4. Al Hemingway, *Our War Was Different: Marine Combined Action Platoons in Vietnam* (Annapolis: Naval Institute Press, 1994), 5–6.
5. Ibid., 172–173.
6. Michael E. Peterson, *The Combined Action Platoons: the US Marines' Other War in Vietnam* (New York: Praeger, 1989), 36.
7. Hemingway, 29.
8. Peterson, 36.
9. Hemingway, 19–20.
10. Peterson, 36.
11. Shulimson, 1966, 240n.

12. Peterson, 46.
13. John Southard, *Defend and Befriend: The US Marine Corps and Combined Action Platoons in Vietnam* (Lexington: The University Press of Kentucky, 2014), 25–26.
14. Hemingway, p. 6.
15. Gary L. Tefler, Lane Rogers, and V. Keith Fleming, *US Marines in Vietnam: Fighting the North Vietnamese, 1967* (Washington, D.C.: US Marine Corps Historical Center, Headquarters, US Marine Corps; 1984), 191.
16. Peterson, 47.
17. Hemingway, 18.
18. Ibid., 44.
19. Ibid., 50.
20. Ibid., 5.
21. Peterson, 48.
22. Ibid.
23. Robert A. Klyman, "The Combined Action Program: An Alternative Not Taken" (Senior honors thesis, University of Michigan, 1986), 24.
24. Peterson,48.
25. Barry L. Goodson, *CAP Mot* (Denton: University of North Texas Press, 1997), 17–18.
26. Ibid., 19.
27. William R. Corson, interview by Michelle Shippen and Ron Greenman, 1984, transcript, U.S. MarineCorps Archives and Special Collections, Quantico, Va.
28. Corson, *The Betrayal*, p. 183.
29. Corson, Shippen and Greenman interview.
30. William R. Corson, interview by Martin Russ, July,1976, transcript, US Marine Corps Archives and Special Collections.
31. William R. Corson, interview by Martin Russ, July 12, 1976, interviews 6313-2A and 6316-A, transcript, Oral History Collection, US Marine Corps Archives and Special Collections

Chapter 7

1. Corson, *The Betrayal*, 184.
2. Ibid.
3. Ibid., 184–185.
4. Ibid., 186–187.
5. Ibid., 187–188.
6. Ibid., 188.
7. Ibid., 188–189.
8. Ibid., 189–190.
9. Ibid., 190.
10. Ibid., 190–191.
11. Peterson, 36–37.
12. Shulimson, 1966, 244.
13. Peterson, 42.
14. Ibid.
15. Igor Bobrowsky, interview, September 11, 1984, Klyman Collection, Folder 7, Box 1, US Marine Corps Archives and Special Collections, Quantico, Va.
16. Peterson, 50.

Chapter 8

1. Michael E. Peterson, *The Combined Action Platoons: The US Marines' Other War in Vietnam* (New York: Praeger, 1989), 32, 50.
2. Robert A. Klyman, "The Combined Action Program: An Alternative Not Taken" (Senior honors thesis: University of Michigan, 1986), 27–28.
3. Peterson, 40.
4. Al Hemingway, *Our War Was Different: Marine Combined Action Platoons in Vietnam* (Annapolis: Naval Institute Press, 1994), 33.
5. William R. Corson, *The Betrayal* (New York: Ace Books, 1968), 276.

6. Gary L. Tefler, Lane Rogers, and V. Keith Fleming, *US Marines in Vietnam: Fighting the North Vietnamese, 1967* (Washington, D.C.:US Marine Corps Historical Center, Headquarters, US Marine Corps, 1984), 259.
7. Ibid.
8. Neil Sheehan, *A Bright Shining Lie: John Paul Vann and America in Vietnam* (New York: Random House, 1988), 641.
9. Lewis Sorley, *Westmoreland: The General Who Lost Vietnam* (New York: Houghton, Mifflin, Harcourt, 2011), 176–177.
10. Ibid., 179.
11. Bui Tin, *From Enemy to Friend: A North Vietnamese Perspective on the War* (Annapolis: Naval Institute Press, 2002), 62.
12. John Prados, *Vietnam: The History of an Unwinnable War, 1945–1975* (Lawrence: University Press of Kansas, 2009), 229–230.
13. Peterson, 56.
14. Hemingway, 59.
15. Peterson, 56.
16. Peterson, 56–57.
17. William R. Corson, interview, Michelle Shippen and Ron Greenman, 1984, transcript, US Marine Corps Archives and Special Collections, Quantico, Va.
18. Ibid.
19. Sorley, *Westmoreland*, 177.
20. Ibid., 182.
21. Ibid., 183.
22. Truong Nhu Tang, *A Vietcong Memoir: An Inside Account of the Vietnam War and its Aftermath* (New York: Vintage Books, 1986), 134–135.
23. James W. Trullinger, *Village at War: An Account of Conflict in Vietnam* (Stanford, CA: Stanford University Press, 1980), 129.
24. Bobrowsky, interview.

25. Peterson, 60.
26. Hemingway, 60.
27. John C.McManus, *Grunts: Inside the American Infantry Combat Experience, World War II through Iraq* (New York: New American Library, 2010), 237.
28. 256 Level, Ralph, interview by Martin Russ, July 16, 1976, interview 6317A, US Marine Corps Archives and Special Collections, Quantico, VA.
29. *Fact Sheet on the Combined Action Force, III Marine Amphibious Force,* March 30, 1970, US Marine Corps Archives and Special Collections, Quantico, VA.
30. Klyman, "CAP", 34.
31. Lewis Sorley, *A Better War: The Unexamined Victories and Final Tragedy of America's Last Years in Vietnam* (New York: Harcourt Brace & Company, 1999), 17–18.
32. Ibid., 23.
33. Robert Coram, *Brute: The Life of Victor Krulak, US Marine* (New York: Little, Brown, and Company, 2010), 319–320.

Chapter 9

1. Peterson, 64, 67.
2. McManus, 223.
3. John Southard, *Defend and Befriend: the US Marine Corps and Combined Action Platoons in Vietnam* (Lexington: The University Press of Kentucky, 2014), 66.
4. McManus, 224.
5. Ibid., 85.
6. Headquarters, Marine Corps, *Small Wars Manual, United States Marine Corps, 1940* (Washington, D.C.: US Government Printing Office, 1940), p. 7.
7. Robert Thompson, *Defeating Communist Insurgency: Experiences from Malaya and Vietnam* (London: Chatto & Windus, 1966), 116–117.

8. Douglas S. Blaufarb, *The Counterinsurgency Era: US Doctrine and Performance 1950 to the Present* (New York: The Free Press, 1977), 258.
9. Trevett, 64.
10. Ibid., 62.
11. Bui Tin, *From Enemy to Friend: A North Vietnamese Perspective on the War* (Annapolis: Naval Institute Press, 2002), 71–72.
12. Richard Nixon, *No More Vietnams* (New York: Arbor House, 1985), 96.
13. John A. Nagl, *Learning to Eat Soup with a Knife: Counterinsurgency Lessons from Malaya and Vietnam* (Chicago: The University of Chicago Press, 2002), 173.
14. Peterson, 81.
15. Ibid., 78.

Conclusion

1. William J. Lederer, *Our Own Worst Enemy* (New York: W.W. Norton & Company, 1968), 229.
2. Robert A. Asprey *War in the Shadows: The Guerrilla in History* (New York: William Morrow and Company, 1994), 949.
3. Douglas Porch, *Counterinsurgency: Exposing the Myths of the New Way of War* (New York: Cambridge University Press, 2013), 324.

Bibliography

Primary Sources

Bobrowsky, Igor, interview, September 11, 1984. Klyman Collection, Folder 7, Box 1. United States Marine Corps Historical Center, Quantico, VA.

Caputo, Philip. *A Rumor of War*. New York: Owl, 1996.

Chau, Tran Ngoc. *Vietnam Labyrinth: Allies, Enemies, and Why the US Lost the War*. Lubbock: Texas Tech University Press, 2012.

Corson, William R. "Phong Bac Hamlet: Case Study in Pacification" 1967, transcript. US Marine Corps Archives and Special Collections. Quantico, Va.

Corson, William R. *The Betrayal*. New York: Ace Books, Inc., 1968.

Corson, William R., interview Russ Martin, July, 1976, transcript. US Marine Corps Archives and Special Collections. Quantico, Va.

Corson, William R., interview by Michelle Shippen and Ron Greenman, 1984, transcript. US Marine Corps Archives and Special Collections. Quantico, Va.

Duong, Van Nguyen. *The Tragedy of the Vietnam War: A South Vietnamese Officer's Analysis*. Jefferson, NC: McFarland & Co., Inc., 2008.

Ek, Paul R., interview, Camp Pendleton, CA, February 10 1966. No. 46, Oral History Collection, US Marine Corps Archives and Special Collections, Quantico, VA.

Paul R. Ek, interview by Jack Shulimson, November 2, 1972. Klyman collection, file 4, Box 1. US Marine Corps Archives and Special Collections, Quantico, VA.

Ek, Paul, interview by Jack Shulimson, 1972. Klyman collection, Folder 7, Box 1. US Marine Corps Archives and Special Collections. Quantico, Va.

Goodson, Barry L. *CAP Mot: The Story of a Marine Special Forces Unit in Vietnam, 1968–1970*. Denton: University of North Texas Press, 1997.

Giap, Nguyen Vo. *People's War People's Army*. New York: Praeger, 1971.

Hemingway, Al. *Our War Was Different: Marine Combined Action Platoons in Vietnam*. Annapolis: Naval Institute Press, 1994.

Huu An, Nguyen. *The New Battlefield*. Hanoi: The Gioi Publishers, 2006.

Krulak, Victor H. "A Strategic Concept for the Republic of Vietnam, June 1965," Klyman Collection, Box#1. US Marine Corps Archives and Special Collections, Quantico, VA.

Krulak, Victor H. "A Strategic Appraisal, Vietnam December 1965". Klyman Collection, Box #1. US Marine Corps Archives and Special Collections, Quantico, VA.

Krulak, Victor H. to Robert S. McNamara, letter, May 9, 1966. Klyman collection, US Marine Corps Archives and Special Collections. Quantico, Va.

Krulak, Victor H. to Paul H. Nitze, letter, July 17, 1966. Klyman collection, US Marine Corps Archives and Special Collections. Quantico, Va.

Ky, Nguyen Cao. *Buddha's Child: My Fight to Save Vietnam*. New York: St. Martin's Press, 2002.

Lee, Alex. *Utter's Battalion: 2/7 Marines in Vietnam, 1965–1966*. New York: Ballantine Books, 2000.

Lehrack, Otto, J., ed. *No Shining Armor*. Lawrence: University Press of Kansas, 1992.

Li, Xiaobing, ed. *Voices from the Vietnam War*. Lexington: University Press of Kentucky, 2010.

Luan, Nguyen Cong. *Nationalist in the Viet Nam Wars: Memoirs of a Victim Turned Soldier*. Bloomington: Indiana University Press, 2012.

Puller, Lewis, Jr. *Fortunate Son: An Autobiography*. New York: Grove, 1991.

Race, Jeffrey. *War Comes to Long An: Revolutionary Conflict in a Vietnamese Province*. Berkeley: University of California Press, 1968.

Santoli, Al, ed. *Everything We Had: An Oral History of the Vietnam War*. New York: Ballantine Books, 1984.

Silva, Lionel. interview by MSC, Quantico, February 2, 1966. No. 37, Oral History Collection. US Marine Corps Archives and Special Collections, Quantico, VA.

Stolfi, Russell H. *US Marine Corps Civic Action Effort in Vietnam, March 1965–March 1966*. Washington, D.C.: Historical Branch, Headquarters US Marine Corps.

Tang, Truong Nhu. *A Viet Cong Memoir: An Inside Account of the Vietnam War and Its Aftermath*. New York: Vintage Books, 1985.

Taylor, Maxwell D. *Swords and Plowshares*. New York: Da Capo, 1972.

Thompson, Robert. *No Exit from Vietnam*. New York: David McKay Company, 1970.

Tin, Bui. *From Enemy to Friend*. Annapolis: Naval Institute Press, 2002.

Wallace, Terry, ed. *Bloods: Black Veterans of the Vietnam War: An Oral History*. New York: Presidio Press/ Ballantine Books, 2006.

Walt, Lewis W. *Strange War, Strange Strategy: A General's Report on Vietnam*. New York: Award Books, 1970.

West Jr., F. W. *The Village*. New York: Pocket Books, 1972.

Westmoreland, William. *A Soldier Reports*. Garden City, NY: Doubleday, 1976.

Zedong, Mao. *On Guerrilla Warfare*. Urbana: University of Illinois Press, 2000.

Secondary Sources

Allnut, Bruce C. *Marine Combined Action Capabilities: The Vietnam Experience*. McLean, VA: Human Sciences Research, Inc., 1969.

Anderson, Jon Lee. *Guerrillas*. New York: Random House, 1992.

Appy, Christian G. *Working Class War*. Chapel Hill: The University of North Carolina Press, 1993.

Appy, Christian G. *Patriots*. New York: Penguin Books, 2003.

Arquilla, John. *Insurgents, Raiders, and Bandits, How Masters of Irregular Warfare Have Shaped Our World*. Chicago: Ivan R. Dee, 2011.

Asprey, Robert B. *War in the Shadows*. New York: William Morrow and Company, 1994.

Baritz, Loren. *Backfire*. New York: William Morrow and Company, 1985.

Blaufarb, Douglas S. *The Counterinsurgency Era*. New York: The Free Press, 1977.

Cable, Larry E. *Conflict of Myths, the Development of American Counterinsurgency Doctrine and the Vietnam War*. New York: New York University Press, 1986.

Callwell, C.E. *Small Wars*. Lincoln: University of Nebraska Press, 1996.

Cann, John P. *Counterinsurgency in Africa, the Portuguese Way of War, 1961–1974*. Westport, CT: Greenwood Press, 1997.

Coram, Robert. *Brute: The Life of Victor Krulak, US Marine*. New York: Little, Brown and Company, 2010.

Daddis, Gregory A. *Westmoreland's War: Reassessing American Strategy in Vietnam*. New York: Oxford University Press, 2014.

Dallek, Robert. *Flawed Giant: Lyndon Johnson and His Times, 1961–1973*. New York: Oxford University Press, 1998.

Davis, Burke. *Marine!: The Life of Chesty Puller*. Boston: Little Brown and Co., 1962.

Dougherty, Kevin. *The United States Military in Limited War*. Jefferson, NC: McFarland and Co., 2012.

Fall, Bernard. *Hell in a Very Small Place*. Philadelphia: J.B. Lippincott Co., 1966.

Fall, Bernard. *Street Without Joy*. Mechanicsburg, PA: Stackpole Books, 1994.

Gaiduk, Ilya V. *The Soviet Union and the Vietnam War*. Chicago: Ivan R. Dee, 1996.

Galula, David. *Counterinsurgency Warfare*. Westport: Praeger, 2006.

Gilbert, Marc Jason, ed. *Why the North Won the Vietnam War*, New York: Palgrave, 2002.

Gurman, Hannah, ed. *Hearts and Minds: A People's History of Counterinsurgency*. New York: The New Press, 2013.

Hammes, Colonel Thomas X. *The Sling and the Stone: On War in the 21st Century*. Minneapolis: Zenith Press, 2006.

Helmer, John. *Bringing the War Home*. New York: The Free Press, 1974.

Henderson, Charles W. *Marshalling the Faithful*. New York: Berkley, 1993.

Hennessy, Michael A. *Strategy in Vietnam: The Marines and Revolutionary Warfare in I Corps, 1965–1972*. Westport: Praeger Publishers, 1997.

Kaiser, David. *American Tragedy: Kennedy, Johnson, and the Origins of the Vietnam War*. Cambridge: Harvard University Press, 2000.

Kilcullen, David. *Counterinsurgency*. New York: Oxford University Press, 2010.

Klyman, Robert A. "The Combined Action Program: An Alternative Not Taken." Senior honors thesis, University of Michigan, 1986.

Klyman, Robert A. "Personal Response Project," box 7, Klyman collection, US Marine Corps Archives and Special Collections. Quantico, Va.

Krepinevich, Major Andrew F., Jr. *The Army and Vietnam*. Baltimore: Johns Hopkins University Press, 1986.

Krulak, Victor H. *First to Fight: An Inside View of the US Marine Corps*. Annapolis: Naval Institute Press, 1994.

Lanning, Michael Lee, and Dan Cragg. *Inside the VC and the NVA, the Real Story of North Vietnam's Armed Forces*. New York: Ivy Books, 1992.

Laqueur, Walter. *Guerrilla: A Historical and Critical Study*. Boston: Little, Brown and Company, 1976.

Lederer, William. *Our Own Worst Enemy*. New York: W.W. Norton, 1968.

McManus, John C. *Grunts: Inside the American Infantry Combat Experience World War II through Iraq*. New York: New American Library.

McMasters, H.R. *Dereliction of Duty*. New York: Harper Collins, 1997.

Millett, Allan R. *Semper Fidelis: The History of the United States Marine Corps*. New York: The Free Press, 1991.

Montgomery, Bernard. *Field-Marshall Viscount of Alamein: A History of Warfare*. London: Collins, 1968.

Moskin, J. Robert. *The US Marine Corps Story*. Boston: Little, Brown, and Company, 1992.

Moyar, Mark. *A Question of Command*. New Haven: Yale University Press, 2009.

Nagl, John A. *Learning to Eat Soup With a Knife*. Chicago: The University of Chicago Press, 2002.

Ninh, Bao. *The Sorrow of War*. New York: Riverhead Books, 1996.

Nixon, Richard. *No More Vietnams*. New York: Arbor House, 1985.

Perks, Robert, and Alistair Thomson. *The Oral History Reader*. New York: Routledge, 2006.

Peterson, Michael E. *The Combined Action Platoons*. New York: Praeger, 1989.

Porch, Douglas. *Counterinsurgency*. New York: Cambridge University Press, 2013.

Prados, John. *Vietnam: The History of an Unwinnable War, 1945–1975*. Lawrence: University Press of Kansas, 2009.

Prados, John. "Strategy in Vietnam: The Marines and Revolutionary Warfare in I Corps, 1965–1972." *The Journal of Military History* 63, no. 2 (Apr. 1999).

Pribbenow, Merle L., trans. *The Military History Institute of Vietnam: Victory in Vietnam, the Official History of the People's Army of Vietnam, 1954–1975*. Lawrence: The University Press of Kansas, 2002.

Ritchie, Donald. *Doing Oral History*. New York: Oxford University Press, 2015.

Sheehan, Neil. *A Bright Shining Lie*. New York: Random House, 1988.

Shulimson, Jack. *US Marines in Vietnam: An Expanding War, 1966*. Washington, D.C.: History and Museums Division, Headquarters, US Marine Corps, 1982.

Shumlinson, Jack, and Charles M. Johnson. *US Marines in Vietnam: The Landing and the Buildups, 1965*. Washington, D.C.: History and Museums Division, Headquarters, US Marine Corps, 1978.

Sorley, Lewis. *A Better War*. New York: Harcourt Brace & Company, 1999.

Sorley, Lewis. *Westmoreland: The General Who Lost Vietnam*. New York: Houghton Mifflin Harcourt, 2011.

Southard, John. *Defend and Befriend: The US Marine Corps and Combined Action Platoons in Vietnam*. Lexington: The University Press of Kentucky, 2014.

Summers, Harry G., Jr. *On Strategy: A Critical Analysis of the Vietnam War*. New York: Dell, 1982.

Tefler, Gary L., Lane Rogers, and V. Keith Fleming. *US Marines in Vietnam: Fighting the North Vietnamese, 1967*.

Washington, D.C.: US Marine Corps Historical Center, Headquarters, US Marine Corps, 1984.

The Marines in Vietnam, 1954–1973: An Anthology and Annotated Bibliography. Washington, D.C.: History and Museums Division, Headquarters, US Marine Corps, 1985.

Thompson, Robert. *Defeating Communist Insurgency: Experiences from Malaya and Vietnam*. London: Chatto & Windus, 1966.

Tierney, John J. Jr. *Chasing Ghosts, Unconventional Warfare in American History*. Dulles, VA: Potomac Books, 2006.

Trevett, Michael F. *Isolating the Guerrilla*. Mustang, OK: Tate Publishing & Enterprises, 2011.

Trullinger, James W. *Village at War: An Account of Conflict in Vietnam*. Stanford: Stanford University Press, 1994.

Turse, Nick. *Kill Anything That Moves*. New York: Metropolitan Books, 2013.

United States Marine Corps. *Small Wars Manual*. Washington, D.C.: United States Government Printing Office, 1940.

Ward, Geoffrey C. and Ken Burns. *The Vietnam War: An Intimate History*. New York: Alfred A. Knopf, 2017.

Weigley, Russell F. *The American Way of War*. Bloomington: Indiana University Press, 1973.

Windrow, Martin. *The Last Valley: The Battle that Doomed the French Empire and Led America into Vietnam*. Cambridge, MA: Da Capo Press, 2004.

Index

A

B

C

J

K

L

M

N

O

P

Q

R

S

T

W